SONGS OF MY PEOPLE

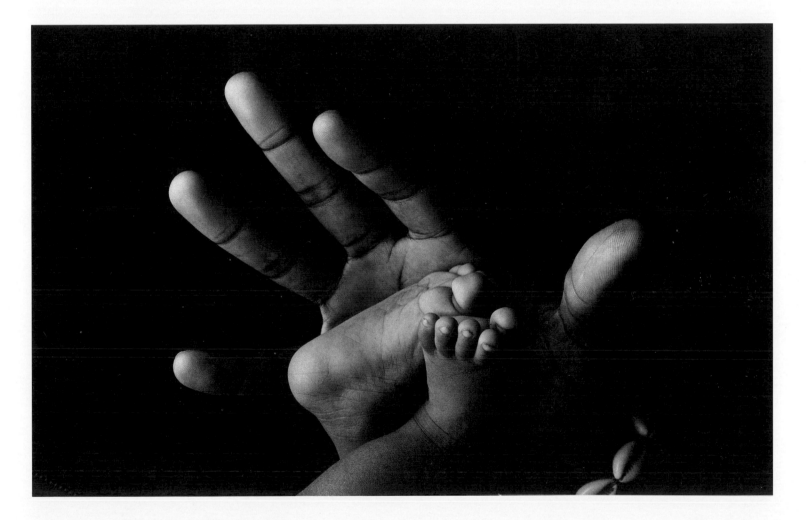

WILMINGTON, DELAWARE

"We of this less favored race realize that our future lies chiefly in our own hands.
On ourselves alone will depend the preservation of our liberties and the transmission of them in their integrity
to those who will come after us." —Paul Robeson

DIXIE D. VEREEN

SONGS OF MY PEOPLE

AFRICAN AMERICANS: A SELF-PORTRAIT

EDITED BY

ERIC EASTER, D. MICHAEL CHEERS AND DUDLEY M. BROOKS

INTRODUCTION BY GORDON PARKS

ESSAYS BY SYLVESTER MONROE, PAULA GIDDINGS,

NELSON GEORGE AND JOYCE LADNER, Ph.D.

LITTLE, BROWN AND COMPANY   BOSTON · TORONTO · LONDON

FIRST EDITION

LIBRARY OF CONGRESS CATALOGING-IN-PUBLICATION DATA

SONGS OF MY PEOPLE : AFRICAN AMERICANS : A SELF-PORTRAIT / EDITED BY

ERIC EASTER, D. MICHAEL CHEERS, AND DUDLEY M. BROOKS : INTRODUCTION

BY GORDON PARKS ; ESSAYS BY SYLVESTER MONROE . . . [ET AL.]. — 1ST

ED.

    P.   CM.

  ISBN 0-316-10966 (HC)

  ISBN 0-316-10981-9 (PB)

  1. AFRO-AMERICANS — PICTORIAL WORKS. I. EASTER, ERIC.

II. CHEERS, D. MICHAEL. III. BROOKS, DUDLEY M. IV. MONROE,

SYLVESTER.

E185.86.S66 1992

973'.0496073'00222 — DC20   91-18933

10 9 8 7 6 5 4 3 2

PUBLISHED SIMULTANEOUSLY IN CANADA BY LITTLE, BROWN & COMPANY (CANADA) LIMITED

PRINTED IN SINGAPORE

< NEW ORLEANS, LOUISIANA

Ezall Quinn, Jr., 10, blows the blues late into the night in the French Quarter.

C. W. GRIFFIN

To my mother, Cynthia M. E. Byrd, and my anchor, Tina T. Hamilton.
Thank you for your love and support. — E E

To my mother, Marie Cheers, I hope you are proud of your son. — D M C

To my family, Amelia J. Brooks, George M. Brooks, Diane Brooks,
Angela, Muriel and Evelyn Brooks, and Dorian Morris Brooks.
Thank you for my values. — D M B

PREFACE

The three of us met for the first time in May of 1989 to discuss producing a book which would tell the story of the African American experience through the unique perspective of African Americans.

In our individual careers as writers and photojournalists, we had had the rare opportunity to cover and be a part of exciting historic moments: the student protests at Tianenman Square in China, the release of Nelson Mandela from a South African jail after 27 years, civil war in Angola, the massive earthquake in Armenia, turmoil in Iraq and Kuwait, the rise and descent of kings, presidents and celebrities.

As African American men, however, we often found the most compelling stories within our own community—in cities large and small, from Brooklyn, New York, and Hattiesburg, Mississippi, to St. Louis, Missouri, and Anchorage, Alaska, there were untold stories of pride, determination, courage, tragedy and triumph. They were stories which demanded to be told, and the best way was through pictures.

It was in that spirit that we created *Songs of My People.*

In the year that it would take to plan and finance the project, we were blessed enough to find a staff of media professionals who shared our vision and helped expand the original concept even further.

During the first week in June of 1990, we flew in 50 of the nation's most gifted African American photographers to Washington, D.C., for a planning meeting at the Corcoran Gallery of Art. We chose an eclectic mix of seasoned veterans

ATLANTA, GEORGIA
Remembering the dream at the Martin Luther King, Jr., Center for Nonviolent Social Change.
E. A. KENNEDY III

and innovative young artists, among them four Pulitzer Prize winners (John H. White, Ozier Muhammad, Matthew Lewis, Keith Williams), two Neiman Fellows (Lester Sloan and Eli Reed), a World Press Award winner (Bob Black), the son of slain civil rights leader Medgar Evers (James V. Evers) and a grandson of the Hon. Elijah Muhammad (Ozier Muhammad). Most in the group had never met before. For many, it was a chance to meet heroes and role models. Indeed, it was the first time such a broad group of African American photographers had come together under the same mission.

On June 3, we handed out assignments, plane tickets and the thousands of rolls of film provided by Eastman Kodak. Over the course of the summer and fall, the photographers traveled from the Atlantic to the Pacific not quite knowing what they would find. We set out not to create a symphony that the photographers would follow note for note, but a jazz composition leaving each artist enough room to improvise and capture what he or she felt.

What they discovered were Black people facing the challenges of a changing nation. They found stories which spoke of our beauty, our achievements, our troubles, our diversity, our African heritage and our American-ness.

They photographed young African American soldiers at boot camp on Parris Island, South Carolina, unknowingly training for a war thousands of miles away. They spent time on the backroads of the South, with farmers in Georgia and Mississippi concerned that by the end of this century they may no longer have land left to farm. They found an overworked doctor in Tchula, Mississippi, who converted an abandoned restaurant into a health clinic serving the entire community. Those who pay, do; those who can't still receive high-quality care. No one gets turned away.

NEW ORLEANS, LOUISIANA

Part of a classic New Orleans tradition, Milford S. Dolliole, a first-line brass-band drummer, is still active.

ROLAND L. FREEMAN

They photographed those who had achieved success beyond their dreams and others who struggle for survival from day to day. One photographer spent a month with one of the rising number of homeless families in American cities. Living on what they can raise on the streets, the family is often uncertain where they will spend each night. The last time the photographer saw them, the Knights were living in an abandoned van.

They witnessed the joy of a couple experiencing the birth of their first child, and the pain of a single mother, addicted to crack, suffering through her third pregnancy and a premature delivery.

They turned their cameras toward the nation's prisons and struggled to understand why more Black men are incarcerated in the United States than in apartheid South Africa. They photographed the streets of Harlem, Los Angeles and Washington, D.C., and found brothers caught up in a world of drugs and senseless violence.

But most of all, they found hope—mothers, strong fathers, families, scholars, athletes, poets, painters, dancers, lawyers, and the faces of children who will determine the future of the world, like Carolyn Michel, the beautiful child on the cover who hopes one day to become a doctor. Ordinary people, living extraordinary lives.

No one picture tells the whole story. Each photograph is a beat in the rhythm of a song yet unfinished—
Songs of My People.

—Eric Easter, D. Michael Cheers, Dudley M. Brooks

TRIANA, ALABAMA
Homerun!
E. A. KENNEDY III

ST. HELENA ISLAND, SOUTH CAROLINA

Siti Opio celebrates her daughter Kemba's graduation from Lloyd's Christian Day Care.

JEFFERY ALLAN SALTER

INTRODUCTION Gordon Parks

Songs of My People is a revelatory window to a world of pulsing Blackness. Sometimes, looking at its pages is like peering through shattered glass; often, at other times, it is akin to squinting through the darkness of a new dawn. Confused eyes, so long retired to the past, will be unprepared for things that, to them, appear unnatural—Black astronauts, symphony conductors, nuns, cowboys, and college students singing hope and promise with their eyes.

With deep thought and imagination, this rare assemblage of photographers picked their stations inside and outside the shadows to give us a vision, that is not really a vision, but a revealing fretwork of Black American life. They strayed into joyful and sorrowed places; into holy places where people praise God; into the privacy of homes; into grief-hung prisons; and into hamlets that exist only on maps. An aged lady's face is there, saying what her lips have left unsaid. The sad eyes of a little girl, lifted toward the lens for a second, reflect the stars on our country's flag, while seeming also to reflect the darkness of the morning wrapped around her. Two children —one Black, one White—hold hands as they swing together. In the innocence of their youth, the air of racial difference loosens as they swing. Looking at them one has the feeling that perhaps America's air is blowing fresher; that at last American hearts are undergoing a needful dusting.

In many ways this is happening. And no other art form has more diligently recorded our painful metamorphosis than the camera. In the proper hands, it burrows deep into feelings of human beings and into the true nature of their conditions.

For these reasons mostly, photography has best served me as a profession. I turned to it with hopes of having a voice that people would have reason to listen to. Because of the frustration that assaulted my early life—prejudice, discrimi-

nation and intolerance—I have attempted to show, through my work, the problems of people around me. There was the responsibility to point up the plight of others less fortunate than myself; to communicate the abuse of the underprivileged as well as the insensitivity of those who administer the abuse. Silent watching was not enough. Even verbal condemnation had to give way to commitment.

Photography was the most accessible way to put commitment into practice. When a *Life* magazine editor asked me why Black people were burning big city ghettos, I pointed my camera at an impoverished Harlem family suffering the brutal hot summers and terrible winters in a decaying tenement. For anyone who seriously wanted to understand the problem, this family's plight was evidence enough. Yet, when my camera became deeply ensnared in their misfortune, my problem was to report objectively—without allowing my subjective feeling to take over completely. The point of issue was to do it simply and honestly so that their predicament would have been as understandable in China, as it was in Missouri or Texas.

But, to many photographers, charged with various aesthetic and emotional impulses, the camera lends a different meaning. Not all are interested in probing the depths of social conditions. To some, the pleasure of capturing beautiful imagery is gratifying enough. I have no quarrel with this. All painters are not concerned with adversity, and all music is not composed for those who like sorrowful songs; otherwise many would not be worth awakening to. I have tried to strike a reasonable balance—to affirm the good and condemn the bad. I loathe the barrios of Puerto Rico and Harlem, and the favelas of South America. I abhor the misery spilling throughout India, Haiti and parts of Africa. Yet, there are things and places of beauty that hold special significance for me. Never am I to forget a great half-ball of African sun rising above Kenya; burning red against a band of Masaii tribesmen, who moved with balletic grace through the dark-green shadows of Mount Kilimanjaro. And there was Paris, for instance, with its ancient buildings, towers and spires jutting gracefully up from the cathedrals. So often my camera has turned from poverty to the ornate bridges along the Seine; to the barges and boats plying the dark silky water flowing beneath them.

At times I have sat at the Café aux Deux Magots on the colorful Left Bank, photographing from where Villon, Balzac or Baudelaire might have sat. Other days, from high above the city of Montmartre, I have focused my lens on the classical Paris of Moliere as it sprawls in the soft light of an evening sky; on Notre Dame, where Napoleon was crowned Emperor. One winter I stood in the vast Kansas prairie land at what seemed to be the still point of the universe. Before me lay a wilderness of dying grass laden with hoarfrost reaching to infinity. Suddenly rays bursting from a rising sun painted the entire expanse a brilliant orange. A school of wild geese winged beneath the rippled sky heading south. For a few unforgettable moments the prairie was a corner of the earth where nature had chosen to show itself at its very best. I have tried to show things as they are: the darkness and the light; the cheerful faces and the disgruntled ones. And what my camera has recorded is, in large part, what I have come to know about our universe and the people who inhabit it. What I have not photographed is what I have yet to see or learn. And I have learned a number of things along the way. Of those I value most is the ability to take human beings as they are, to take measure of them; to accept or reject them regardless of their skin. I have learned not to expect any more, or less, from a Black stranger than I would a White one. It all depends upon the stranger. Like my family, my friends represent such a huge pastiche of hues; I no longer assign them to colors. They are friends, and that is more than enough. They could hardly be called homogeneous—Blacks, Chinese, Jews, Germans, Irishmen, and a Southerner from Louisiana. Altogether, they are like one big sheltering tree with different colored leaves. That is the way things are, and I do not welcome any change.

I have never gloried at being the first Black director in Hollywood, the first Black photographer to work at *Vogue, Life* or other such places. I like to feel their doors were opened for my race as well as for me. I did realize that I was making fresh tracks, but I never carried the responsibility around on my back like a sack of stones. I simply did my best without asking for favors because I was Black. Time and again those tracks have been filled by other Blacks, and for me this is reason to rejoice.

I have painful memories of having endured those poison markets that hamper and subjugate racial groups in this country. Recalling my own experience is like looking back on a sequence of burned squares wherein people wrapped hatred around me like tangleweed and attempted to impede my growth—unyielding, insensitive people obsessed with the belief that Blacks, Indians and Mexicans were meant to live as second-class citizens. Many hapless victims died keeping their silence. Perhaps I was born with a stubbornness that my tormentors failed to take into account. The injustices they heaped upon me engendered my craving to escape their intolerance with the help of a camera.

Covering some of the stories in the past three decades was like reporting from the darkness. During that time I saw men in incomprehensible actions against their fellow men. I

witnessed jagged moments of brutality and terror. I came to understand the implication of bigotry, poverty and war. During some unbelievable hours I doubted that another morning would arrive; each day seemed sufficient to bring the world to a stop.

Nonetheless, I have been in awe of what remained to be admired. For while evil and corruption suited certain people, there were others inclined toward greatness, the good ones who refused to be squashed under the heels of others. These, when the sky threatened to fall upon us, raised their voices and guaranteed us another sunrise. And there were beautiful things to see—so beautiful they defy description. I recall gazing from a Colorado mountaintop down toward a winding river that boiled with foam, thinking simply that God had created yet another truly awesome sight.

This collection of photographs by Black photographers of mostly Black people speaks for itself. I think of it as an inward look. The heart, not the eye, seems to have determined the contents of their photographs. What their eyes saw was one thing; what their hearts perceived was yet another.

All of the contributors were born to a childhood of confusion, because they were born Black. Obviously the hopes, fears and trials of their lifetimes influence their work. And this is as it should be. One sees clearly that they have transcended the limitations that might have been wrongly ascribed to their birthright. They have witnessed deplorable things still happening around them and, with their cameras, attempted to help squash them.

In helping one another we can ultimately save ourselves. We need miracles now, I am afraid. If only we could understand the needs of our past, then perhaps we could anticipate our future. We cannot get too comfortable in our houses. The hawk of intolerance still hovers in the air, and restless bigots still talk bigotry in their secret rooms.

Songs of My People is Black music lifting, falling, flowing beneath the undercurrents of love, uncertainty, happiness and despair. Its rhythm rises and falls with a cadence that is often intense and reflective; at times romantic and discordant—but always desperate with a need to be felt deeply. The images evolve from shadows over which the light of the universe falls—showing us who we Black people are, what we should be, or hope to become. The turning of these pages furnishes its own applause, and as the pages turn, your heart may wince, smile or speak bitterly to itself. It might nudge you into an extraordinary view of your own conscience that could make you blink or gasp. The images pile up against one another, heightening our awareness, bringing us to understand the time into which we were born; why, as time passes, we must nourish a need to excel through the wealth of our African heritage.

ST. HELENA'S ISLAND, SOUTH CAROLINA A brief rest. **JEFFERY ALLAN SALTER**

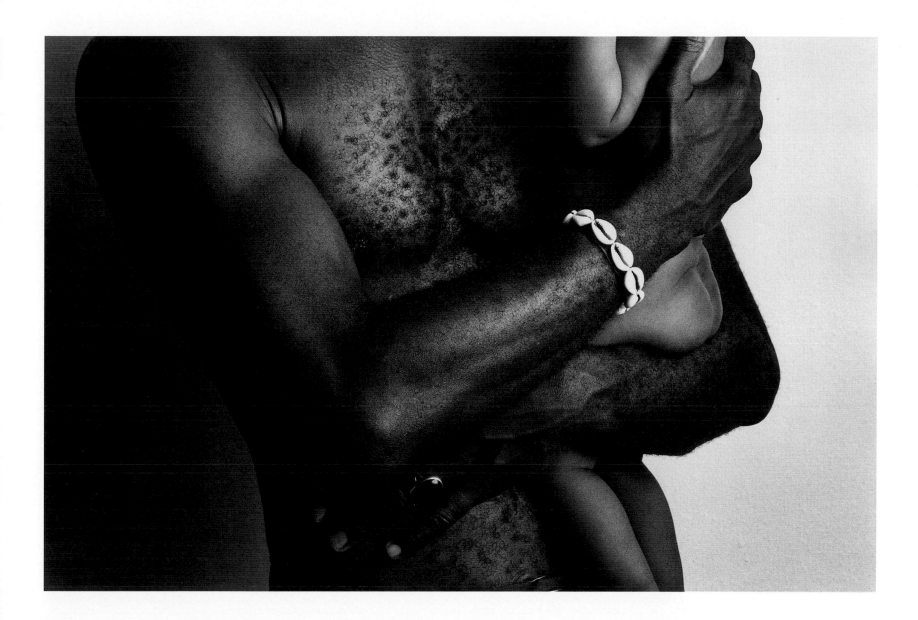

WILMINGTON, DELAWARE   Man and Child.   **DIXIE D. VEREEN**

NEW YORK, NEW YORK

A subway musician plays the harmonica for commuters in a
Greenwich Village station.

CONRAD BARCLAY

BALTIMORE, MARYLAND
City High School's 20th anniversary reunion at 32nd Street Plaza nightclub.
DUDLEY M. BROOKS

BALTIMORE, MARYLAND
Waiting for the bus at Pratt and Light Streets.
DUDLEY M. BROOKS

NEW ORLEANS, LOUISIANA

Jazz greats of the future: The Little Rascals

featuring Ezall Quinn, Jr., Terrence, Eldridge and Larry Andrews, and Corey Henry.

ROLAND L. FREEMAN

PHILADELPHIA, PENNSYLVANIA
Urban Bush Women, a multi-arts theatre ensemble,
performs contemporary pieces about Afrocentric traditions and lifestyles.
JULES ALLEN

NEW ORLEANS, LOUISIANA   Love in the French Quarter—a bench kiss.   **ROLAND L. FREEMAN**

CHICAGO, ILLINOIS   Early morning.   **BOB BLACK**

BROOKLYN, NEW YORK   Waiting for a haircut.   **DAVID LEE**

BROOKLYN, NEW YORK

Watching the neighborhood change, on Malcolm X Boulevard in Bedford-Stuyvesant.

DAVID LEE

NEW ORLEANS, LOUISIANA

Sam Blakely has worked for 20 years at the French Market.

C. W. GRIFFIN

BROOKLYN, NEW YORK   The neighborhood.   **DAVID LEE**

NEW YORK, NEW YORK
Leading fashion designer Gordon Henderson and model Melanie Landestoy,
wearing Henderson's designs.
GEORGE CHINSEE

< **CHICAGO, ILLINOIS**   Cooling off.   **BOB BLACK**

MILWAUKEE, WISCONSIN   A facelift.   **BOB BLACK**

WASHINGTON, D.C.   >
The old Howard Theater was once the centerpiece of Black Washington until the riots of 1968.
With a new subway line coming in, the neighborhood hopes for a revitalization.
JASON MICCOLO JOHNSON

TCHULA, MISSISSIPPI
Alice W. Smith makes feeding the neighborhood kittens a daily ritual.
D. MICHAEL CHEERS

DAUFUSKIE ISLAND, SOUTH CAROLINA

Louise Wilson, 71, a sixth-generation Daufuskie Islander, feeds chickens outside the Wilson home.

JEFFERY ALLAN SALTER

SHELDON, SOUTH CAROLINA
A strong connection to the Motherland led a group of African Americans to build "Oyontunji" village
and follow the traditions of the Yoruba people of southwestern Nigeria.
T. ORTEGA GAINES

<   **WASHINGTON, D.C.**
Aziza Ali and her constant companion, "Dolly Ali," after Moslem prayer services at the Washington Masjid.
RON CEASAR

McROBERTS, KENTUCKY Dodge ball in the Appalachian Mountains. **DURELL HALL, JR.**

NEW ORLEANS, LOUISIANA   Hide and seek.   **C. W. GRIFFIN**

DAUFUSKIE ISLAND, SOUTH CAROLINA

Innocence.

JEFFERY ALLAN SALTER

McROBERTS, KENTUCKY >

At sunset, the electric wires over McRoberts glisten.

DURELL HALL, JR.

VITAL SIGNS:
THE BLACK MALE

Sylvester Monroe

Phillip Eugene Morris was born on June 8, 1990, in Santa Monica Hospital. His mother, Marita Jackson, a 29-year-old nurse's aide, lives in Long Beach, California. His father, Reginald Morris, Sr., 36, owns a security company in Gardena. They are not married. For now, they say, marriage is not in the cards.

A day later, on June 9, Carrington Xavier Greene was born in Howard University Hospital in Washington, D.C. His parents, Quintin A. Greene, 33, an exhibit manager at a D.C. children's museum, and his mother, Sophia, 29, a budget assistant at Howard, also have a four-year-old daughter, Naomi. They are a normal, working-class Washington family.

Though they come from different circumstances, live on opposite sides of the country and have never met, like most parents, Morris and Jackson and the Greenes hold high hopes for their brand new baby boys. Morris, who grew up in a fatherless home and does not communicate with a 15-year-old son from a broken marriage of his own, hopes Phillip will be the cornerstone of a reconstructed Morris clan. Greene wants Carrington to get a better education than the two years of college he managed and to enjoy a better communicating relationship with him than he had with his father.

The parents also share a common burden and a growing national concern: raising Black male children in a nation where to be young, Black and male is tantamount to being an endangered species. Statistics supporting this now-familiar claim

PIKE COUNTY, KENTUCKY
James Shelton, Jr., has worked the Kentucky coal mines for 18 years. He is one of only 15 Black miners left in the small town of 650.
DURELL HALL, JR.

are alarming at best, a threat to the health and well-being of all Black Americans at worst. From cradle to grave, the numbers show that Black males consistently languish on the bottom rung of America's socioeconomic ladder.

Black male babies, for example, are twice as likely as White babies to die in the first year of life, and more than three times as likely to be born weighing less than three pounds. Indeed, in 1987, the gap between Black and White infant mortality was the widest ever recorded and growing. A similar racial disparity afflicts Black males at the other end of life. While White Americans live an average of six years longer than Blacks as a whole, the life expectancy of Black males, 65.1 years, is far shorter than the 78.9 years of White females, 73.8 years for Black females or even the 72.1 years for White males. In fact, while longevity for most Americans has remained at record high levels, the life span of Black males actually declined between 1987 and 1988. Black men in Harlem, for example, are less likely to live to 65 years old than men in Bangladesh—one of the poorest countries on earth. The promise of life in between infancy and old age is not much better. Increasing numbers of Black American males face a bleak existence characterized by lagging levels of educational achievement, employment and family stability.

If indeed a Black boy survives the infant mortality gap, he will quickly confront his next major hurdle—systematic low expectation of teachers—in practically any school system from Washington to Watts, Detroit to Dallas. A recent survey in New Orleans, for example, revealed that six out of ten teachers said they did not believe their Black male students would make it to college. Sixty percent of those were elementary school teachers, and most startling of all, 65 percent were Black. The results of such negative attitudes are often

self-fulfilling prophecy. While Black males represented 43 percent of the New Orleans school system, they accounted for 58 percent of the students with failing grades, 65 percent of the suspensions, 80 percent of the expulsions and 45 percent of the dropouts.

Not only are a Black boy's chances of attending college much slimmer than his White American counterpart, he is, in fact, much more likely to go to jail or be killed than to go to college at all. Again, the statistics are astonishing. One of every four Black men in his twenties is either in jail, in prison, on probation or on parole. And more Black men in their twenties are under court control than there are Black men of all ages in higher education. In California, Black males are three times as likely to be murdered than to be admitted to the University of California. By contrast, only about eight percent of White men in that age group are incarcerated or under court supervision, and more than four times as many White men are in college than are under court control. Even worse, between the ages of 15 and 25, a Black male is ten times more likely to be a murder victim than if he were White.

Unfortunately, avoiding premature death and attending college do not significantly increase a Black male's chances of escaping second class status in American society—compared to Whites. Black men still are two and a half times as likely to be unemployed as Whites, and even middle class Black males earn considerably less than same status White males. And the trend is worsening. The current $10,000 gap between Black and White middle class male incomes is double what it was in 1973.

No wonder that when Sophia and Quintin Greene discovered she was pregnant with their second child, Sophia silently prayed it would be another girl. Not surprisingly, Reg-

inald Morris and Marita Jackson are fearful for their son, too. Morris is particularly concerned that Phillip does not succumb to the same set of social diseases—broken family, social isolation and gang violence—which have all but consumed his other son, Reginald, Jr., a hopelessly lost man-child of 15, whose sole allegiance is to the L.A. street gang he considers his only family.

Acutely aware of the limited life chances available to Black males, both couples have vowed to go to any length to protect their sons. Exactly how they will prevent them from joining the grim statistics reflecting what finally has been recognized as a national crisis is a matter of growing debate. While the Greenes plan to leave the nation's drug-plagued capital for the safer surroundings of South Carolina, Morris and Jackson are prepared to pack up and move as far from the gang-riddled streets of L.A. as Texas or Tennessee. Others, taking a different approach, have suggested that young Black boys be segregated from other students and taught in special Black-males-only classes and schools.

Ultimately, solutions to the Black male crisis lie neither in family relocation nor in the isolation of Black boys. Racism, discrimination and the perpetuation of negative, stereotypical images of Black males have contributed enormously to the problem and remain ever-present facts of life for the society into which Carrington Greene and Phillip Morris were born. Those evils, no matter how overt or insidious, must continue to be fought at every turn. Moreover, Black parents and Black adults in general must accept both a large part of the blame

for allowing the problem to have become so critical and the lion's share of the responsibility for solving it.

Indeed, it is Black parents, first and foremost, who must give young Black boys (and girls) the love, support and sense of self-worth that can only come from family. Black parents must teach Black youth the true, long-lasting value of education and provide role models and constant guidance so they understand and believe that just because they cannot sing a love song like Michael Jackson or dunk a basketball like Michael Jordan does not mean they cannot rise above the self-destruction of crack and crime.

It is Black men who must inspire Black boys to want to be the Malcolms, Martins and Mandelas of the future. Black men must show young Black males that even when society seems to place little or no value upon their lives, they still have a stake in it. Above all else, Black men must teach Black boys how to be men. They must pass on to Black boys the same hope Black women have traditionally passed to Black girls. And they must teach Black boys to dream, to see beyond the probabilities of life to the possibilities.

DETROIT, MICHIGAN

Willie T. Ribbs of the Raynor-Cosby racing team in the pit at the Detroit Grand Prix.

He continues the family legacy of professional racing started by his father, Bunny.

Ribbs was the first African American driver to qualify for "Indy" car racing.

KENNETH WALKER

WASHINGTON, D.C.

Secretary of Health and Human Services Louis Sullivan in his office.

The only African American cabinet member in the Bush administration, he is also an avid chess player.

JASON MICCOLO JOHNSON

NEW YORK, NEW YORK

In 1980, Ralph Wright became the first Black specialty broker on the New York Stock Exchange.

EZIO PETERSEN

BATON ROUGE, LOUISIANA

At 24, Cleo Fields became the youngest person elected to the office of state senator in America.

Now 28, he has his sights on national office.

C. W. GRIFFIN

LOS ANGELES CALIFORNIA

Andre Tweed, M.D., 76, the first Black certified psychiatrist in California,

worked on several famous criminal cases, including that of the Manson family.

His professional success allowed him to amass a museum-quality collection of African art.

LESTER SLOAN

NEW YORK, NEW YORK >

Black photography pioneer Roy DeCarava is inspired by the scenes outside his Brooklyn window.

CHESTER HIGGINS, JR.

ATLANTA, GEORGIA

Reginald Askew and James Day work high atop
Atlanta on what will be its tallest skyscraper.

E. A. KENNEDY III

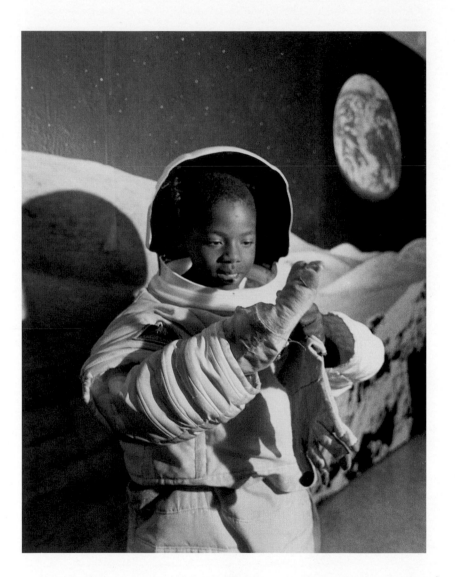

HUNTSVILLE, ALABAMA

Ten-year-old Eric Spurlock's dreams of becoming an astronaut led him to the summer Space Camp

run each year by the National Aeronautics and Space Administration (NASA).

A little closer to his dream, Eric takes a ride on the ⅙ Gravity Simulator.

E. A. KENNEDY III

BLACK COWBOYS

CLEBURNE, DALLAS, AND LONGVIEW, TEXAS
Shortly after newly freed slaves began migrating westward, Black folks were involved in horseback riding for sport as well as business. Legendary rodeo star Bill Pickett, who pioneered the art of "bulldogging," was unstoppable back in 1904. In 1971, he became the first African American inducted into the National Rodeo Hall of Fame. Today, African Americans continue to enjoy the pastime.

KEITH WILLIAMS

EAST ST. LOUIS, ILLINOIS

Like many industrial towns across the nation, an ever-changing economy

transformed a once-booming East St. Louis into a city with shutdown factories and boarded housing.

Yet many of its unemployed residents, like David James, maintain hope for the city's comeback.

ODELL MITCHELL

LOS ANGELES, CALIFORNIA

Libby Tracy, 17, (foreground) lives in Jordan Downs in Watts, an area police call "the most dangerous zone in the city."

Bucking pressure to be a gang member, Tracy is a good student who scored high on his SAT.

On his 17th birthday, a week after being recruited by a Missouri college, he was arrested on suspicion of assault.

After a weekend in jail, the charges were dropped.

D STEVENS

LOS ANGELES, CALIFORNIA

Gang activity in south central Los Angeles is not a game, but an unfortunate and dangerous reality.

One brother threw up his gang symbol for this photograph.

D STEVENS

LOS ANGELES, CALIFORNIA

George Thomas is a resident of the notorious Imperial Courts housing project in south central L.A.

According to Thomas, "The projects are like a war zone—a twilight zone.

It's only a matter of time before you become a victim. I would love to be living when the book comes out . . ."

D STEVENS

BROTHERS
BEHIND
BARS

SUGARLAND, TEXAS

A 1990 survey produced a sobering statistic: one out of four Black males was in prison or under court supervision. Among the many were these men incarcerated in the Texas Department of Corrections Central Unit.

GEARY G. BROADNAX

SUGARLAND, TEXAS

Some brothers remain hopeful about their opportunities once they are paroled. Others may never get out.

GEARY G. BROADNAX

TRANSFORMATION

PARRIS ISLAND, SOUTH CAROLINA

This 6,000 acre island off the coast of South Carolina is where the United States Marine Corps "transforms" young men and women into soldiers.

Since the Revolutionary War, African Americans have fought and died bravely and heroically in defense of freedom, ironically something not always afforded them at home.

Today, African Americans represent more than 30 percent of the United States armed forces.

JEFFERY ALLAN SALTER

PARRIS ISLAND, SOUTH CAROLINA

Recruit Gavin Vanier gets a lesson in hand-to-hand combat.

JEFFERY ALLAN SALTER

PARRIS ISLAND, SOUTH CAROLINA

Drill instructor Sgt. Pugh Curtis teaches recruits how to use the bayonet.

JEFFERY ALLAN SALTER

HOPE

ATLANTA, GEORGIA

At age 13, Terrance Singh was electrocuted and severely burned when his hand touched an electrical wire while he was dangerously riding atop a train. To save him, doctors had to remove both his legs. Every day presents a challenge as Singh attempts to overcome his handicap. In Atlanta, swimming instructor Salaam Green agreed to help.

RENEE HANNANS

HEALING

BALTIMORE, MARYLAND

Walker Robinson, M.D., is chief of neurosurgery and pediatrics at the University of Maryland Baltimore Shock Trauma Unit. Robinson began his day performing successful reconstructive head surgery on a nine-month-old. The boy suffered from hydrocephalus, also known as "water on the brain," a condition which is often fatal within the first year of life if untreated.

DUDLEY M. BROOKS

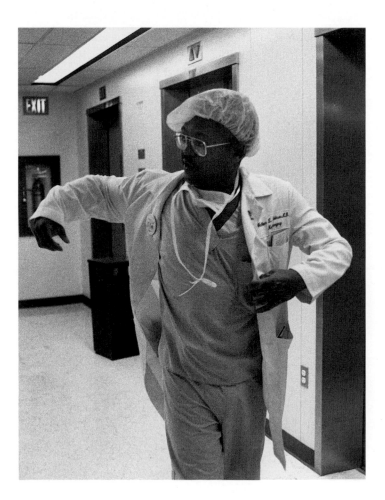

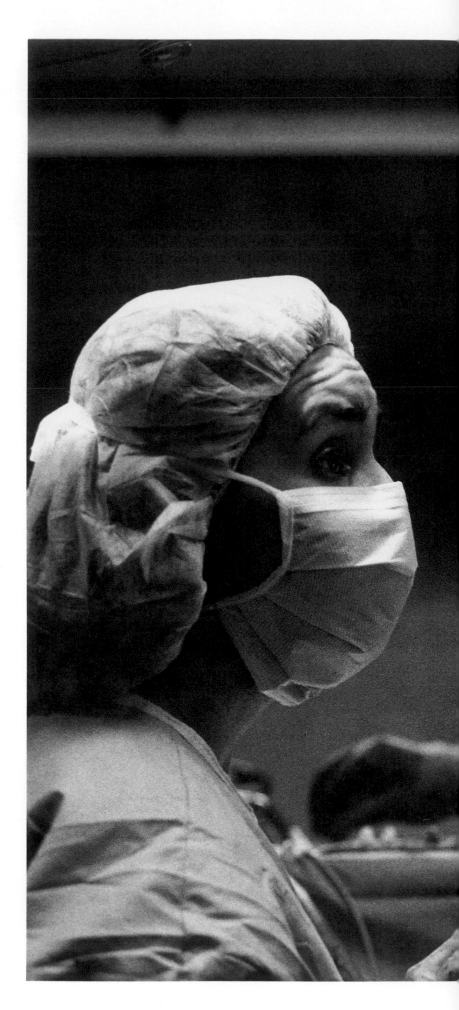

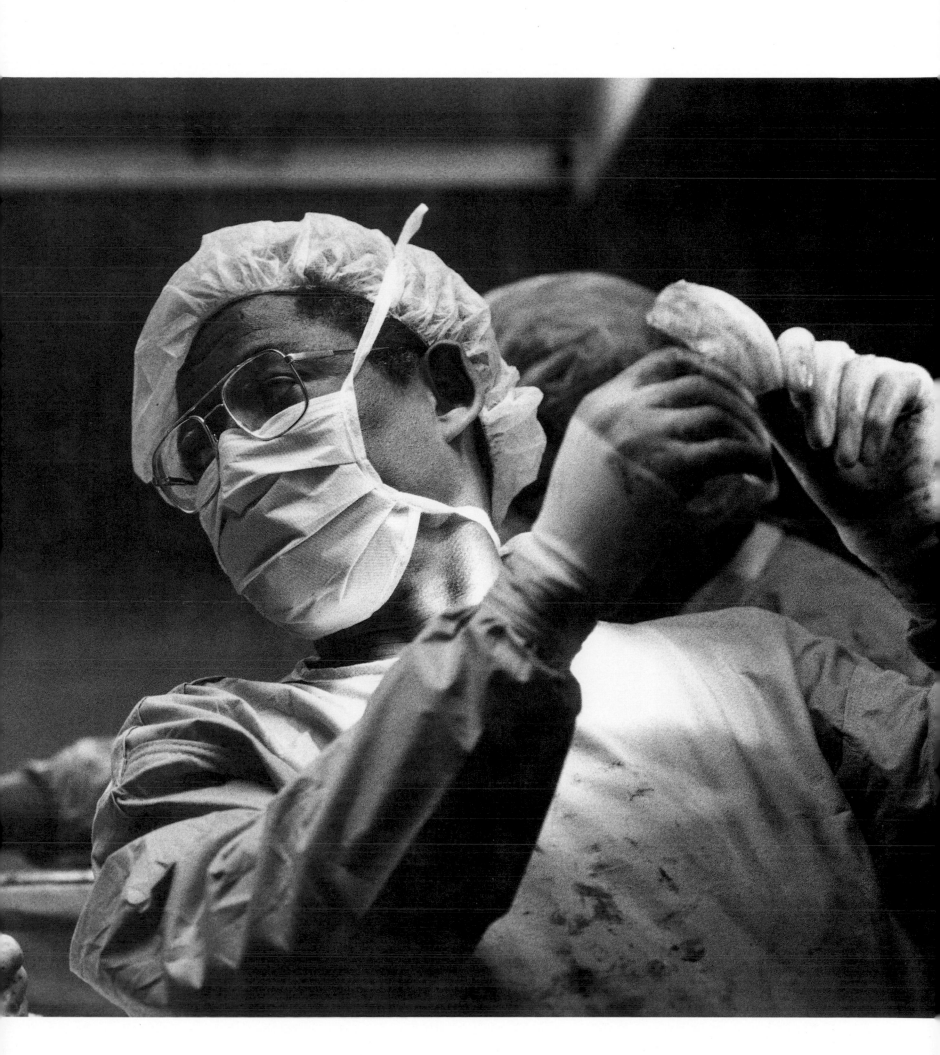

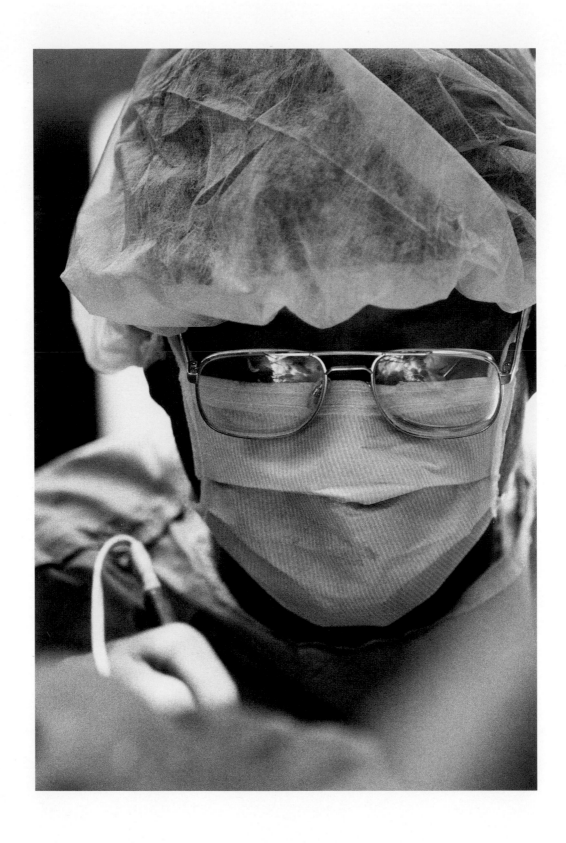

BALTIMORE, MARYLAND

Performing hundreds of operations each year, Dr. Robinson literally holds the lives of others in his hands.

DUDLEY M. BROOKS

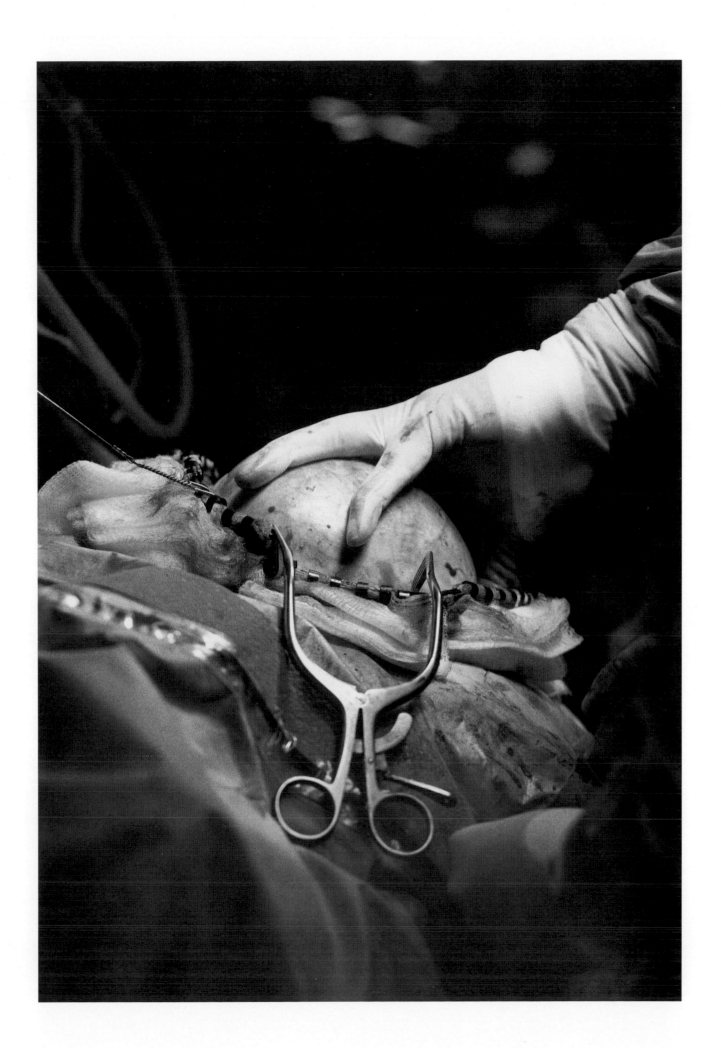

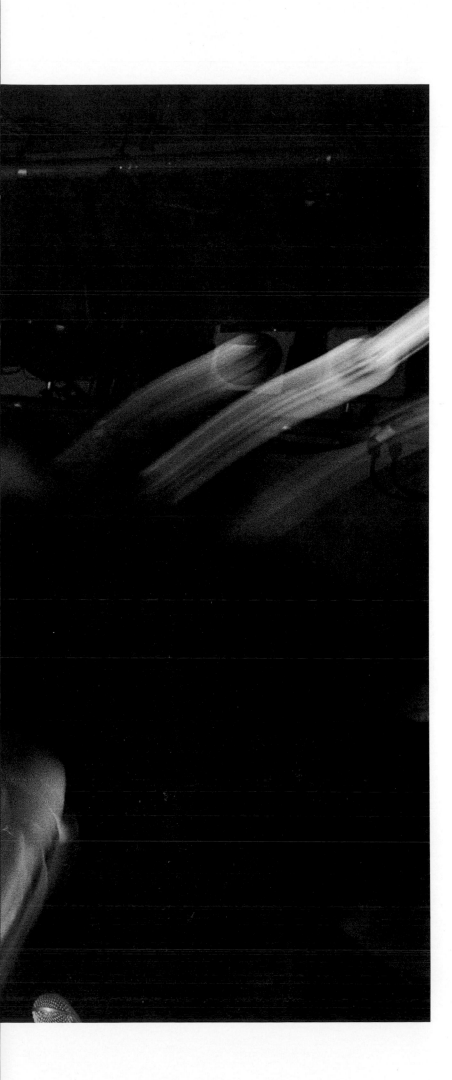

BOYZ AND GIRLZ IN THE HOOD

Nelson George

It is Summer 1990, and the artists are not on vacation. At 43rd and Degnan in Los Angeles' Crenshaw section is the Crossroads Arts Center. Funded by television star Marla Gibbs and run by another Black television favorite, Whitman Mayo, Crossroads is a place where young people from the surrounding area—be they from the neat homes of Baldwin Hills or the working class developments locals call "the Jungle"—are taught the art of acting. On a hot afternoon in one of Crossroads' little theaters, six young women work through pantomime exercises for their acting teacher, translating everyday experience into that heightened reality known as art. In another part of the Crossroads complex, an interracial team of filmmakers sits behind computer screens and telephone banks. Under the guidance of bespectacled 23-year-old University of Southern California film school graduate John Singleton, they are preparing to make a film titled *Boyz in the Hood.* Singleton, a native of south central L.A., has drawn from his life as well as that of family and friends, to create a multi-layered tale of a Black Los Angeles never before depicted in a major feature film. With the clout of Columbia Pictures behind him, Singleton is preparing to put the world—his world—on celluloid.

At the same time, a mere 3000 miles away, Spike Lee sits in the converted Fort Greene firehouse that houses his company, 40 Acres and A Mule Filmworks, consulting with his brilliant cinematographer Ernest Dickerson and actor Wesley Snipes about *Jungle Fever,* a film about miscegenation in

NEW YORK, NEW YORK
"Bigga," a reggae band from Florida, jams at SOB's (Sounds of Brazil) nightclub in Manhattan.
CONRAD BARCLAY

LOS ANGELES, CALIFORNIA
Filmmaker John Singleton.
D STEVENS

NEW YORK, NEW YORK
Around midnight, jazz saxophonist Stanley Turrentine puts
his soul into his music at Sweet Basil nightclub.
CONRAD BARCLAY

cation. Fort Greene is a compact little neighborhood near the northern tip of Brooklyn that in the 1980's blossomed into a Black arts colony. At any given hour some of African America's most famous artists toil steadily to make a dream come alive. In Crenshaw, for decades a center of Black life in the city of Los Angeles, Gibbs, Mayo and Singleton have all made a commitment of time and money to giving something back to a place and a people who have nurtured their careers.

Finally, all these artists, and the thousands working in communities between Fort Greene and Crenshaw, are co-workers in the job of translating the joy and pain of the African tenure in America into scripts, songs, characters, paintings, poems, and sundry other artistic expressions.

Some would argue that the continuing existence of African Americans in the United States, given the genocidal racism of the majority population, shows that our race has mastered life's most important art—the art of survival. On a more benign level the cultural products of the African American are, at their best, both a protest and a celebration of that survival instinct. In the 1990's, just as in every other decade of this fast-fading century, it is our art that is central to shaping perceptions of this nation. The millions of dollars generated by Black culture are a tangible representation of African-Americans' ability to entertain, inform, and inspire. But it all starts in the 'hoods where Mayo gives instruction, Singleton learns, Lee operates, and Rock finds humor. Everyday, in places like the Crossroads Arts Center or a Fort Greene brownstone, away from the bright lights and autographs, African American art is being constructed by women and men who are building on a firm foundation of community.

It is summer and the artists aren't on vacation. Why? Because our art never stands still.

a racially torn New York City. And Lee, Dickerson and Snipes aren't the only people on a mission in this brownstone-laden Fort Greene area. A few blocks away singer Alva Rogers rehearses her unique blend of soul, rock and opera for the pending recording of her debut album. A block further, comic Chris Rock scribbles jokes into a spiral notebook. He's about to join the cast of "Saturday Night Live," and Rock plans on having his game together before that first broadcast airs.

Gibbs, Mayo, Singleton, Lee, Dickerson, Snipes, Rogers and Rock are African Americans linked together, not merely by the craft of entertaining, but also by the idea of community in a variety of senses. As African Americans they partake in the long, rich and constantly evolving culture of their people. A spirit of national community binds them in ways both tangible and mystical, a spirit that manifests itself in dance steps and slang words, handshakes and haircuts—and in unspoken ways that can be felt like whispers in the heart.

This spirit of community is partially a by-product of lo-

LOS ANGELES, CALIFORNIA
The Dude. Renowned composer, arranger, producer, and multi-media company chief Quincy Jones.
Here, Jones plays a character in a light-hearted music video.
JAMES V. EVERS

< **CHICAGO, ILLINOIS**
Michael Morgan, the first Black assistant conductor for the Chicago Symphony Orchestra, was the first to integrate the company.
He also serves as music director of the Oakland East Bay Symphony in Oakland, California.
BOB BLACK

THE WOODLANDS, TEXAS

Jazz, born in the heart of the Black community, is regarded as America's greatest cultural contribution.

One of its pioneers, trumpeter Miles Dewey Davis, continues to inspire and influence contemporary music in all its forms.

GEARY G. BROADNAX

NEW YORK, NEW YORK
Legends: The Daddy of the Blues meets the King of Rock and Roll. John Lee Hooker (left) and Bo Diddley (right).
JACQUES CHENET

NEW YORK, NEW YORK
Bassist Ray Drummond holds down the rhythm.
ANTHONY BARBOZA

< **LOS ANGELES, CALIFORNIA**
Trumpeter Lester Bowie plays jazz on the cutting edge.
ANTHONY BARBOZA

MINNEAPOLIS, MINNESOTA

Since the emergence of groups like Prince and The Time, Minneapolis has become a central point on the New Music scene.

Gary Hines, a producer at Flyte Tyme Studios, helps carry on the tradition.

EARL ANDERSON

NEW YORK, NEW YORK

Rap group X-Clan represents part of the increasingly popular Hip Hop movement
which has grown out of a renewed awareness of African heritage and community pride.

CONRAD BARCLAY

WASHINGTON, D.C.
George Goodman plays guitar in front of Union Station every day to the pleasure of passersby.
DUDLEY M. BROOKS

WASHINGTON, D.C. >
Tap dance artist Johnne Forges performs at Cafe Lautrec twice weekly where he dances on the bar.
DUDLEY M. BROOKS

ATLANTA, GEORGIA
Happy hour at the Parrot Cabaret, where singles mingle.
E. A. KENNEDY III

< **ST. PAUL, MINNESOTA**
Folks dance on Monday nights at Everybody's, a Black-owned nightclub that features a range of music from disco to jazz.
EARL ANDERSON

PHILADELPHIA, PENNSYLVANIA

Bernice Collins is a dancer with the Ringling Brothers circus.

A native of Kansas, she was attracted to circus life by dancing, travel and the close family of performers.

JULES ALLEN

PHILADELPHIA, PENNSYLVANIA
Since age 12, Huell Speight wanted to be a circus clown.
A ten-year veteran of the Ringling Brothers and Barnum and Bailey Circus, he loves the way children react.
"First, they're afraid; then they smile. When I finally break the ice—that's special."
JULES ALLEN

LAS VEGAS, NEVADA

Showgirls in their dressing room at Bally's Casino Resort. Bally's was one of the first hotels to integrate its showgirl line.

KENNETH WALKER

SEATTLE, WASHINGTON

On the heels of the Harlem Renaissance, Jacob Lawrence began to make his mark in the world of fine art.

With the backing of the Works Project Administration (WPA) of the Federal government,

he got the financial boost he needed—one which catapulted him and his work into international renown.

BRUCE TALAMON

FOLK ARTIST

ROCKVALE, TENNESSEE

Eighty-six-year-old Alvin Jarrett is a woodcarver who spends much of his day on his porch forming tools, utensils and novelty items from cedar. Some of the wood he uses was cut by his ancestors and resurrected for his carvings.

CRAIG HERNDON

NEW YORK, NEW YORK

A whimsical look at the foods that have nurtured African Americans—

watermelon, ham hocks, collard greens.

COREEN SIMPSON

WASHINGTON, D.C.

The lights are always on at the Capitol Pool Checker Club.

The club has nearly 60 members—all who take their game very seriously.

JASON MICCOLO JOHNSON

ST. HELENA ISLAND, SOUTH CAROLINA

Christy Moultrie, a member of Gray's Hill Clipperettes Softball team, practices for a game with the Coastal Rent-All team.

JEFFERY ALLAN SALTER

DETROIT, MICHIGAN

Ringer!

PAT WEST

LOS ANGELES, CALIFORNIA

L.A. Raiders' Art Shell, the first Black NFL head coach in modern times, keeps a watchful eye from the sidelines.

KIRK McKOY

< **NEW YORK, NEW YORK**

Carrying on the tradition of tennis great Althea Gibson, top-ranking player Zina Garrison
holds her own on the women's professional circuit.

STEVE LEFKOVITS

CHICAGO, ILLINOIS
Brothers play a pick-up game of basketball at midnight on Chicago's South Side.
BOB BLACK

LOS ANGELES, CALIFORNIA >
Basketball superstar Isiah Thomas takes his shot in a dunking contest
for the charity Midsummer's Night Magic All-Star Game, sponsored by Los Angeles Laker Magic Johnson.
HOWARD BINGHAM

LOS ANGELES, CALIFORNIA

At Muscle Beach, many young brothers work out in between showing off for the women on the boardwalk.

LESTER SLOAN

DETROIT, MICHIGAN

Still "floating like a butterfly," former heavyweight champion Muhammad Ali stays in shape at his home gym.

HOWARD BINGHAM

A FIGHTING CHANCE

BROOKLYN, NEW YORK
The Bedford-Stuyvesant section of Brooklyn has a slogan, "Do or Die, Bed-Stuy."
That's also the motto of the New Bed-Stuy Boxing Center.
ELI REED

BROOKLYN, NEW YORK

Founded in 1979 by former flyweight champion Henry "Hot Pepper" Brent as an alternative to the streets,
the center has turned out Olympic champions like welterweight Mark Breland and heavyweight Riddick Bowe.

ELI REED

BROOKLYN, NEW YORK

The coaches teach the students, ages 8 and up, how to turn boundless energy into abundant skill.

ELI REED

BROOKLYN, NEW YORK

Says Mitchell Pendleton, the center's director,

"We want the discipline they learn here to translate into their personal and professional lives.

We want them to know that they can be whatever they want to be."

ELI REED

KENNER, LOUISIANA

The Reverend Clarence Vinnett in front of Solid Rock Non-Denominational,
the church he started in his backyard ten years ago.

C. W. GRIFFIN

CHICAGO, ILLINOIS >

African Americans have brought a soulful heritage to the Catholic Church.
A revival at St. Sabina Catholic Church is full of spirit.

BOB BLACK

NEW YORK, NEW YORK

Brass bands are an integral part of the worship service at the United House of Prayer for all People in Harlem.

OZIER MUHAMMAD

MIAMI, FLORIDA

One Sunday each month, the children of St. Mary's Catholic Church in Little Haiti perform a traditional dance.

KEITH HADLEY

CHICAGO, ILLINOIS

Albertina Walker, widely known as the "queen" of gospel music, in concert.

BOB BLACK

WASHINGTON, D.C.

The Reverend Joan A. King gives praise on a Sunday morning at Metropolitan African Methodist Episcopal Church.

JASON MICCOLO JOHNSON

McROBERTS, KENTUCKY
The Reverend Laurence Hollyfield, assistant pastor of the Church of God Militant Pillar and Ground of the Truth
in rural Appalachia, delivers the word. He doubles as a coal mine foreman.
DURELL HALL, JR.

PHILADELPHIA, PENNSYLVANIA   >
Passing the plate at Mother Bethel AME, the birthplace of the African Methodist Episcopal Church
and the site of the oldest land consistently owned by Blacks in the United States.
MARILYN NANCE

PHILADELPHIA, PENNSYLVANIA   Sunday best.   **MARILYN NANCE**

<   **NEW YORK, NEW YORK**
Sunday mornings at Abyssinian Baptist Church bring out sisters in hats.
COREEN SIMPSON

NEW ORLEANS, LOUISIANA
Priest Oswan Chamani practices the voodoo religion in the French Quarter.
C. W. GRIFFIN

DETROIT, MICHIGAN

Another side of the champ: Muhammad Ali and his family, devout Moslems, pray toward Mecca.

HOWARD BINGHAM

ST. LOUIS, MISSOURI

Steven Cousins and Sandra M. Moore grew up in the same neighborhood. Though they went separate ways as adults, their experiences with racism and discrimination led them both to the legal profession. After 20 years, they rekindled their friendship. Moore is now an administrative judge for the Equal Employment Opportunity Commission and Cousins is a nationally recognized attorney who specializes in corporate bankruptcy.

D. MICHAEL CHEERS

TRIANA, ALABAMA

Looking forward to the day when he is old enough to vote, Nick Fletcher, son of Triana Police Chief Joe Fletcher,
peers through a window next to a voting booth. Prior to the passage of the Voting Rights Act of 1965,
Nick would only have been able to dream about exercising his right.

E. A. KENNEDY III

< **WASHINGTON, D.C.**

By the time he was appointed by President Lyndon Johnson to the United States Supreme Court in 1967,
Associate Justice Thurgood Marshall had already secured his place in history.
As a young attorney Marshall was a major force behind the victories in groundbreaking civil rights cases,
including *Brown v. Topeka Board of Education*.
The first African American to serve on the nation's highest court, he has created an enduring legacy.

JASON MICCOLO JOHNSON

WASHINGTON, D.C.
Joint Chiefs of Staff Chairman General Colin Powell and First Lady Barbara Bush enjoy a dance
at a reception for Black appointees to the Bush Administration.
JASON MICCOLO JOHNSON

MACON, GEORGIA

Former Atlanta Mayor Andrew Young and wife Jean on the road during his 1990 bid to become Georgia's first Black governor.
Though he lost the race, he was successful weeks later in helping to deliver the 1996 Summer Olympics to Atlanta.

E. A. KENNEDY, III

NEW YORK, NEW YORK

New York City Mayor David N. Dinkins inspires school children at Gracie Mansion.

EZIO PETERSEN

WASHINGTON, D.C.

With a pledge to "clean house," in 1990 Sharon Pratt Dixon became the first African American female mayor of a major city.

SHARON FARMER

MARTHA'S VINEYARD, MASSACHUSETTS

Dorothy West, 80, an essayist from the Harlem Renaissance period, still writes short stories.

VINCE FRYE

SISTERS STAND STRONG   Paula Giddings

When I look into the faces of older Black women, I think about my grandmother and the generations before her. I think about the journey that has been our history. It is a journey measured by the stretch of years between now and 1619 when we stepped so unknowingly onto a land called Virginia. It is a journey measured in almost 300 years of slavery, each year strung one to the other, binding us all in an inextricable knot. It is a journey as long as that taken by Harriet Tubman that began in the slave South and ended, triumphantly, at the farthest tip of the North Star.

The journey has been long, and hard too. I see in our hands that only Black women were expected to "work the ground" and, even in freedom, were deemed "de mule of da worl." It was hard to be subjected to the whims of pampered women, and the probings of privileged men. It is even harder to forgive.

But I don't see these things in the eyes of older Black women. I do see, whatever their own lives have been, a kind of eternal hope for us and our children. My grandmother and her friends, all born around 1900, were certainly like that. They were always looking toward the horizon.

After all, my grandmother's mother had been a slave who lived long enough to see freedom. She told my grandmother what newly freed men and women were capable of accomplishing. My great grandmother saw Black men hold political offices from U.S. Senator to local sheriff throughout the South. She saw what the abolitionist Frances Ellen Harper, who toured the South after Emancipation, documented. Blacks, Harper wrote, "were beginning to get homes for themselves, . . . and depositing money in the bank." Black women workers conducted labor strikes for better wages, formed mutual aid societies, enrolled in elementary schools and universities like Howard. By the 1880's, the first Black women had passed the bar to become lawyers; and Black women became the first women, of any color, to practice medicine in the South.

They also fought. When White Supremacists threatened to regain power in Charleston, South Carolina, after Reconstruction, an eyewitness reported seeing Black women "carrying axes or hatchets in their hands hanging down at their sides, their aprons or dresses half-concealing the weapons." By 1892, Ida B. Wells, a 30-year-old Black woman and journalist living in Memphis, Tennessee, began the modern civil rights movement when she launched the nation's first anti-lynching campaign.

Black women also knew that they could form effective organizations. In 1896, they organized the National Association of Colored Women, which would have 50,000 members within a decade and bring forth such leaders as Mary Church Terrell and Anna Julia Cooper, as well as create programs of self-help, aid to the community and women's suffrage that became models for those of the National Association for the Advancement of Colored People (NAACP) and the National Urban League founded later.

Black women undoubtedly knew that they could work. By 1910, as W.E.B. Du Bois wrote in *Darkwater,* Black women "furnished a million farm laborers, 80,000 farmers, 22,000 teachers, 600,000 servants and washerwomen, and 50,000 in trades and merchandizing."

With new opportunities during the World War I years, hundreds of thousands of those women, my grandmother among them, took hope in their hands, wrapped it gingerly and slipped it into their pockets for the journey North. North, where there were jobs in the industrial labor force, where

field work did not keep children out of school, where disenfranchisement, sexual exploitation, and violence at least knocked before entering.

North, where my grandmother unwrapped hope and put it shining on the mantel. It was there where she finished high school, played the organ for church every Sunday, put my mother through college on the wages of domestic work.

During the 1920's, she heard about the Harlem Renaissance and its search for cultural roots, attended the funeral of singer Florence Mills, tried the new hairstyles and outrageous fashions, despaired over the new surge of racial violence. During the Depression, she scrimped meager savings (my mother has never shaken some of those habits); during the 1940's and 1950's, she indulged me after school when my mother picked me up in the sliver of time between the end of one job and the beginning of another.

In these heady years, my grandmother's hopes for her daughter were buoyed by the new opportunities for Black women in the public school system (where my mother worked), civil service and clerical pools which made middle-class dreams possible. (In fact, it was not until Black women had such opportunities after World War II that enough Black families earned the income to constitute a middle class.) Then, as today, the status of women as wage earners had an extraordinary impact on the income of the Black family. Yes, there was celebration in the air during the 1940's. Not only had the percentage of Black women working as domestics decreased from 60 percent to 42 percent, but we were being recognized as federal appointees (Mary McLeod Bethune), front-line organizers for the NAACP (Ella Baker, Ruby Hurley, Rosa Parks, Daisy Bates), prize-winning writers (Gwendolyn Brooks, Margaret Walker) and visual artists (Elizabeth Catlett) as well as in more traditional occupations.

By 1954, a younger generation hoped that the *Brown v. Topeka Board of Education* Supreme Court decision would be the clincher to all this progress. Racist resistance, the realization that economic progress was being eroded even as it was being documented, first stunned Black America, then catalyzed it into action. During the 1960's, Black America marched, inspired, burned, quarreled, lobbied, mourned, masculinized, shouted "Black Power," and celebrated the passage of the Civil Rights and Voting Rights Acts of 1964 and 1965.

My grandmother, in her sixties at the time, didn't say very much about all of this. Nor did she comment on my militant poetry, burgeoning Afro, praise of Motown, or talk of liberation. I thought it was because she wasn't in touch. It

took me a long time to realize it was because she had seen it all before. She had seen cycles before, and she was already at peace with it. What other explanation could there be for the transformation of fire and steel into the soft, sweet playfulness, the gentle care-giver that became my, our, grandmothers?

What would she think of us now? Her eyes would be clear, would register the continuing racism and sexism, the despair, the drugs, the crowding of women into low-paying occupations, the struggle for the hearts and minds of our children. Yet, for every unhappy word we uttered, she would shake her head in disbelief and say:

Look at all the conveniences you have. What it took me all day to do, you can do in minutes. And the opportunities, the choices! You are the first generation of women who can demand the same positions and salaries as men, White or Black; demand the same justice as anyone and not be laughed at. Seems to me the rest is up to you. But you also have to do things that we didn't have to. You have to create new communities for yourselves, your families. I lived in segregated communities because we had no choice about it. So when the choices came, they broke apart. You have to put them back together again, maybe not in the same way, maybe not with all the same people, but you must fashion a place where you can mend, and plan, and not be on guard, and trust each other again. You need a place, concrete or immaterial, where you can take hope out of your pockets and face the world from a position of strength. Seems to me the visions could start right here.

DAUFUSKIE ISLAND, SOUTH CAROLINA

Yvonne Wilson, eight months pregnant, rides the one-trip-per-day "Mary C" ferry to Hilton Head
to her doctor on Hilton Head Island.

JEFFERY ALLAN SALTER

DAUFUSKIE ISLAND, SOUTH CAROLINA
After a clean bill of health, Wilson spends a quiet moment at home.
JEFFERY ALLAN SALTER

BROOKLYN, NEW YORK

Jessica Tuit, 11, wants to be a ballet dancer. She takes lessons at
the American Dance Theater for the Deaf.

MICHELLE AGINS

HOUSTON, TEXAS >

In 1985, Sandra Organ became the first African American soloist
for the Houston Ballet.

MARK GAIL

WASHINGTON, D.C.

When these shots were taken, Beatrice Fergerson, 97, had mastered the art of the hula-hoop.

SHARON FARMER

SAVANNAH, GEORGIA

Renita "Buffy" Lipscomb, an Armstrong State College student, crams for a final exam.

JEFFERY ALLAN SALTER

BALTIMORE, MARYLAND

At one of the oldest historically Black colleges, Morgan State University, graduates celebrate.

DUDLEY M. BROOKS

NEW YORK, NEW YORK

Mother Clare Hale at Hale House says: "We don't take any money from the city . . .
they try to tell us how to take care of these babies. I've been caring for these children for 21 years.
Now the city wants us to separate the HIV-positive babies from the others, and I refuse. We give them all love."

BRUCE TALAMON

NEW BEDFORD, NEW YORK

At 70, former jazz singer Beverly Hodge is the "mother" of New Bedford Women's Correctional Center.
Serving a life sentence for murder, she is sought out by her fellow inmates for comfort and advice.

JEANNE MOUTOUSSAMY-ASHE

THIS FAR BY FAITH

CATONSVILLE, MARYLAND

The Oblate Sisters of Providence have been reaching out to the African American community for more than 160 years. Founded in 1829 by Sister Mary Elisabeth Lange, a freed slave from the Dominican Republic, the order was the first to welcome women of color into the cloth.

DIXIE D. VEREEN

CATONSVILLE, MARYLAND
Despite years of discrimination, the Oblate Sisters remain strong today,
dividing their time between educating young people in the area and conducting the business of the convent.
DIXIE D. VEREEN

CATONSVILLE, MARYLAND
But the average sister in the order is 69, and youthful prospects are not yet knocking on the door.
DIXIE D. VEREEN

WASHINGTON, D.C.
Shades of beauty.
DUDLEY M. BROOKS

<   **LOS ANGELES, CALIFORNIA**
Atallah Shabazz, actor and activist, is the oldest daughter of the late civil rights leader Malcolm X.
KIRK McKOY

NEW YORK, NEW YORK

Since the high fashion color line was broken in the late 1960's, Black models have helped redefine beauty around the world.

Standing (left to right): Renauld White, Veronica Webb, Rashid Silvera.

Seated: Cynthia Bailey, Peggy Dillard and Wanakee.

GEORGE CHINSEE

BROOKLYN, NEW YORK

Saturday morning at the beauty salon.

DAVID LEE

CHEYENNE, WYOMING

As opportunities for women grow, more African American women choose the armed forces to develop their skills.

At F. E. Warren Air Force Base, Myra Cross is the only female photographer.

MORRIS RICHARDSON

WASHINGTON, D.C.

Doctors Karen Ambrose, Paula A. McKenzie, and Deborah Arrindell practice the healing art for Kaiser Permanente in Maryland.

D. MICHAEL CHEERS

WHITHER THE BLACK FAMILY? Joyce Ladner, Ph.D.

The Black family evokes strong sentiments in most Americans. Its very mention conjures up images of thousands of slaves stacked on top of each other in overcrowded ships during the Middle Passage. It evokes the harsh images of slave owners with bullwhips beating rebellious Black men who refused to submit to the authority and role of this inhumane system and of Black women screaming as their children were torn repeatedly from their breasts as they were about to be sold to another plantation.

The Middle Passage, slavery, Reconstruction, and the subsequent mass migration North to the inner city tenements—that is the Black family. Yet the Black family is a diverse institution consisting not only of the impoverished plantation to inner city individuals living on the edge of poverty, but also of those Black freedmen and women who were euphemistically referred to as "house servants." Often the sons and daughters of White plantation owners who sired them by Black slave women, this small group of people formed the core of the Black middle-class elite that persists to the present. This diverse Black family ranges from those whose great-grandparents were educated at elite White institutions to the downtrodden of the so-called "underclass."

These disparate Black families are united by a common cultural bond: the legacy of Africa, slavery, and subsequent experiences in the New World that forged within them all a sense of being both American and Black, of having two war-ring identities—according to W.E.B. Du Bois—irreconcilable in one body that is torn asunder.

Where has the Black family come from? Where is it at present? Where is it headed?

To answer the first question is to suggest that the Black family is the only family system in America that has had to endure the hardships of slavery. Blacks were denied the most basic rights accorded to families. They were considered to be three-fifths of a man—denied the right to vote and to own property and thereby to inherit the same; denied the right to practice their own native religions and allowed only to practice Christianity under the watchful eye of White slave holders; denied the right to be educated; and denied the right to marry and thereby to bear children in wedlock.

Somehow Black men and women were not to be deterred by these severe denials. Not content to pray exclusively to an unknown God, they added the remnants of their own culture which they had imported from Africa to these foreign shores. Most important, they forged a family system from the bits and fragments of opportunities available to them. Hence, Black men and women "jumped the broom" as they celebrated the marriage ritual in lieu of not being able to obtain a marriage license from the state. They passed on the names of other family members to their infant sons and daughters who, although technically born illegitimate, were nevertheless legitimate in the eyes and hearts of their slave parents. When slavery ended, Black men and women crowded the dusty southern roads as they searched for the families from which they had been separated. The proof that slaves had not been stripped of their African cultural heritage, with its high regard for the importance of family, was borne out by the fact that in the decades immediately following the abolition of slavery,

MACON, GEORGIA
Because Shontee Deshazier was promoted to the fifth grade, her grandfather, Robert Smart, treated her to lunch downtown.
E. A. KENNEDY III

marriage rates soared. Husbands and wives who had "jumped the broom" but had been separated found their way back to each other, proving that no matter what hardships suffered under the laws of segregation, strong family values endured.

The notion that Black families could be reunited following slavery is a testament to their resilience. Through the good times and the bad, the family has endured not only hardships, but boundless successes as well. The devotion to hard work, fortitude, and an unshakable faith in God, as well as to the uplift of the race have fortified the traditions that kept the family together. Racial discrimination, instead of being solely a barrier, was often the glue that held extended families and communities together. Segregated institutions restricted opportunities, but they also bound Blacks together in tightly knit survival units. The segregated communities gave families a sense of purpose, an identity, and a strong sense of unified values. Segregated schools, churches, and other institutions strengthened family values instead of working against them. Middle-class and poor families alike were rich in traditions and values, purpose and identity, goals and common strivings to do well. "We didn't know we were poor until someone told us," said a woman, describing her family life in the segregated South.

Poverty alone did not determine life's chances. It was the rich texture of life itself that added immeasurably to one's outcomes. But there have been a great many changes in our families over the past 20 years.

A generation ago, divorce was frowned upon and scorned in our communities; today if a man and woman decide to separate, it's nobody else's business. Abortions, illegal then, are now legal, and contraceptives (once not even mentioned in polite conversation) can be bought at the local convenience store. Our grandmothers and neighbors once took care of our children when we worked or needed a break; today, too often, our youngsters live latchkey or are put in child-care centers. Our elders, before the respected source of family traditions, now are often isolated from those who once depended on them for their wisdom. The demands of modern living—long work hours and little leisure time—have forced many of us to place our elderly relatives in nursing homes or senior-care centers.

At the same time, in the last 20 years we have also excelled. We have produced our share of social workers, teachers, bankers, and business professionals. More of our people are going to college and entering careers once closed to us; now we are found in virtually every occupation—from Supreme Court justice to astronaut.

Yet others of us remain trapped in a fragile mobility that limits our climb up the economic ladder and makes it hard for those of us who have made it to stay put on our rung. Many Blacks are just one paycheck away from poverty, and most have reached middle-class status only by having two wage earners in the family; if one partner gets sick or loses a job, they run the risk of a backward slide.

Much of the above, however, is a description of the Black family before it began the current changes and transition it is experiencing. The family, for the past 20 years, has experienced a steady erosion of the tried-and-true formulas for its success. A worsening economy has had adverse effects on the ability of the poor to provide for family needs. Blacks, having a disproportionately higher rate of poverty, are among the major losers in this downward economic spiral. Families have been beset not only by a recessionary economy, but by a plethora of social problems as well. Crime and violence,

BILOXI, MISSISSIPPI
Vacation on the beach.
JOHN H. WHITE

teenage child-bearing, housing shortages, inadequate educational opportunities and health care have severely weakened the infrastructure of poor Black families. The rise in female-headed households is linked to the decline of productive roles for men in families. The worsening economic problems perhaps have had a more severe impact on poor Blacks than any other group of Americans. The numbers of Black children living in poverty increased at an alarming rate over the past 15 years, causing many children to suffer more than children in developing countries. High rates of infant mortality and morbidity, communicable diseases, inadequate diets, poor education and housing are having a profoundly negative impact on the ability of these children to grow into healthy, productive adults.

Despite these problems, two-thirds of Black families are not living in poverty. Most families have made unprecedented gains in income and education, housing, and other opportunities. Middle-class parents who are first-generation college-educated now enjoy the same opportunities to provide the finest material advantages of their White counterparts to their children. Today Black students excel at Howard and Harvard Universities. Unlike their parents' generation, they are no longer confined legally to Black institutions. And many Black families have exploited these new resources to their advantage, rising out of abject poverty to join the middle class in only one generation.

These economic and educational opportunities have created a solid Black middle-class family that stretches the entire expanse of this nation. Members of this class are astronauts, corporate executives, college presidents, lawyers, doctors, teachers, and preachers. Still many are subjected to the invisible glass ceiling which restricts their upward mobility. Racial discrimination keeps Black lawyers carrying briefcases from getting taxis in New York City and Washington, D.C., while Black middle-class female shoppers are still mistaken by Whites to be saleswomen in department stores.

Overall, the middle-class Black family has done well, but there is still a distance to go. The more acute problems are those facing the one-third of Black families living in poverty. The erosion of the economy—steel mills, automobile factories, manufacturing—has displaced a significant number of Blacks from their jobs. Additionally, the transition to a high technology, service-based economy has caused further erosion in the lives of Blacks who do not have the education and training to get those jobs. Social problems, such as drugs and violence, add to the problems. Still the Black family continues to be bound by its strong heritage—its resilience in the face of racism and poverty, its resourcefulness, its optimism, its ability to endure, and its faith in the future.

PROM NIGHT

CHICAGO, ILLINOIS

One of many rites of passage that we remember years later, either with trepidation or delight,
Prom Night represents that transition from being a child to somehow being "grown up."

BOB BLACK

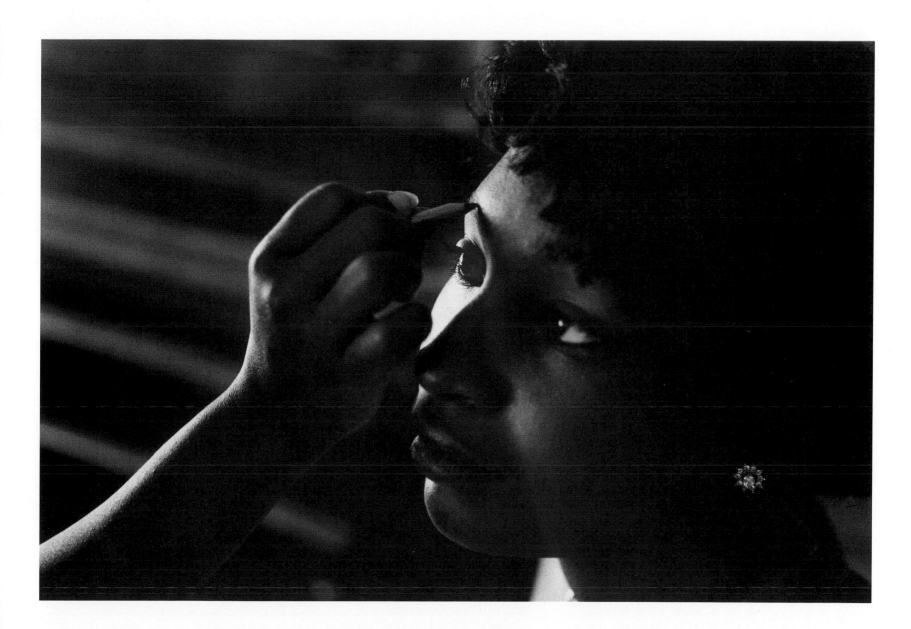

CHICAGO, ILLINOIS

Preparation for the big night is as much an occasion as the event itself.

There's shopping for dresses, renting tuxedos, applying makeup, and pinning the corsage.

BOB BLACK

CHICAGO, ILLINOIS

Family and friends join in to help Stevie Black and his sister Crishon ready themselves

for the magical entrance into the next stage of their lives.

BOB BLACK

BATON ROUGE, LOUISIANA
Latasha Augustus, 10, tests the laws of gravity in Spanish Town Park.
C. W. GRIFFIN

< **WASHINGTON, D.C.**
Ernest Hicks, a security officer at the Department of Defense and a law student at night,
shares time with his children before going to work.
DUDLEY M. BROOKS

HARDEEVILLE, SOUTH CAROLINA
Rites of passage: A light.
JEFFERY ALLAN SALTER

< **BROOKLYN, NEW YORK**
A haircut.
DAVID LEE

SHARING

SAN FRANCISCO, CALIFORNIA

Though both are professionals with high-stress jobs, Dr. Gene Washington and his wife, Marie, an investment
banker, still find quality time to spend with their three children, Brooks, Caroline and Erin.

BRUCE TALAMON

ST. LOUIS, MISSOURI

Vernon Wellington quit his job at a major St. Louis construction company to start the Wellington Building Group
with his wife, Jacqueline. Their company's first contract was for $29,000 to construct a bus shelter.
In 1990, they were named associate construction managers of a new $250 million stadium complex.
The project represents the largest construction contract awarded an
African American firm in the history of St. Louis.

D. MICHAEL CHEERS

HOUSTON, TEXAS

Up to the point of his untimely death in a plane crash in Ethiopia,

Representative Mickey Leland of Texas spent his life helping the poor and hungry.

Now his widow, Allison Leland, instills his legacy in their three sons, Jarret, Austin and Cameron.

GEARY G. BROADNAX

CHICAGO, ILLINOIS

Jesse Louis Jackson, Jr., is congratulated by his father, Jesse, Sr., and mother, Jacqueline,

at his graduation from Chicago Theological Seminary.

JOHN H. WHITE

ATLANTA, GEORGIA

Saturday morning chores. The whole family joins in.

KEITH HADLEY

HOLDING ON

PRINCE GEORGES COUNTY, MARYLAND

James and Lonise Bias have lost two promising sons, Len and Jay, to drugs and senseless violence.
Through it all they have remained strong, turning their personal pain into a nationwide campaign
for community involvement and nonviolence.

<   More than 3,000 people attended the funeral for Jay Bias. A friend says a prayer at the coffin.

RON CEASAR

SURVIVAL

WASHINGTON, D.C.

David Knight has two years of college training in computer science, but says he can't "get a five-dollar-an-hour job at a fast food restaurant." When their government-subsidized building was closed because of health code violations, the Knights moved into a city-operated shelter for the homeless.
Conditions worsened, and the Knights left. David became depressed and was unable to keep his part-time job.

D. MICHAEL CHEERS

WASHINGTON, D.C.

During the day, David looks for work, while his wife, Joyce, and their two-year-old grandson, Jamal,

panhandle near the entrance to a subway station two blocks from the White House.

A "good day," says Joyce, will bring in about $20.

D. MICHAEL CHEERS

WASHINGTON, D.C.
During the month that this story was photographed, the Knights found shelter
in the basement of an apartment building, a friend's home and a van.
D. MICHAEL CHEERS

WASHINGTON, D.C.
Jennifer and Marc Loud "jump the broom."
ROY LEWIS

NEW ORLEANS, LOUISIANA

Jean-Paul and Bernadette Pinel own an art gallery in the French Quarter.

ROLAND L. FREEMAN

BIRTH

Vincent Reynolds shares the wonders of childbirth with his wife, Donna.

Nichelle Aviane was born at Holy Cross Hospital on August 8, 1990, at 6:39 p.m., weighing in at a healthy 7 pounds, 15 ounces.

D. MICHAEL CHEERS

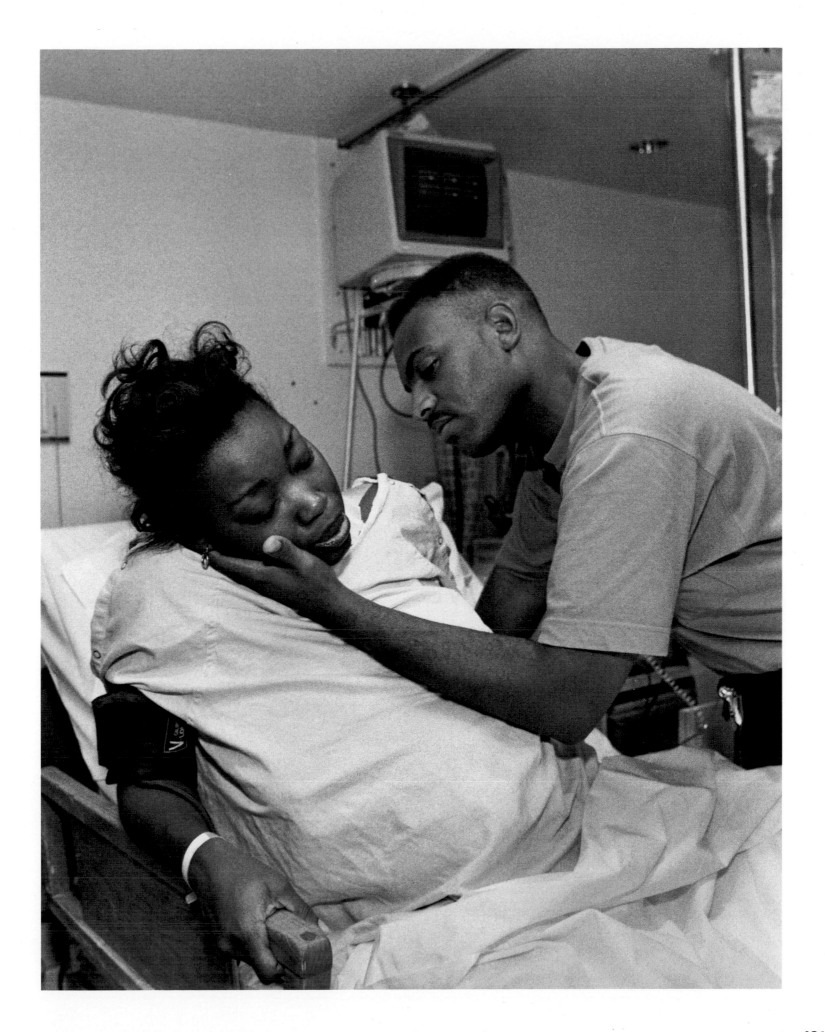

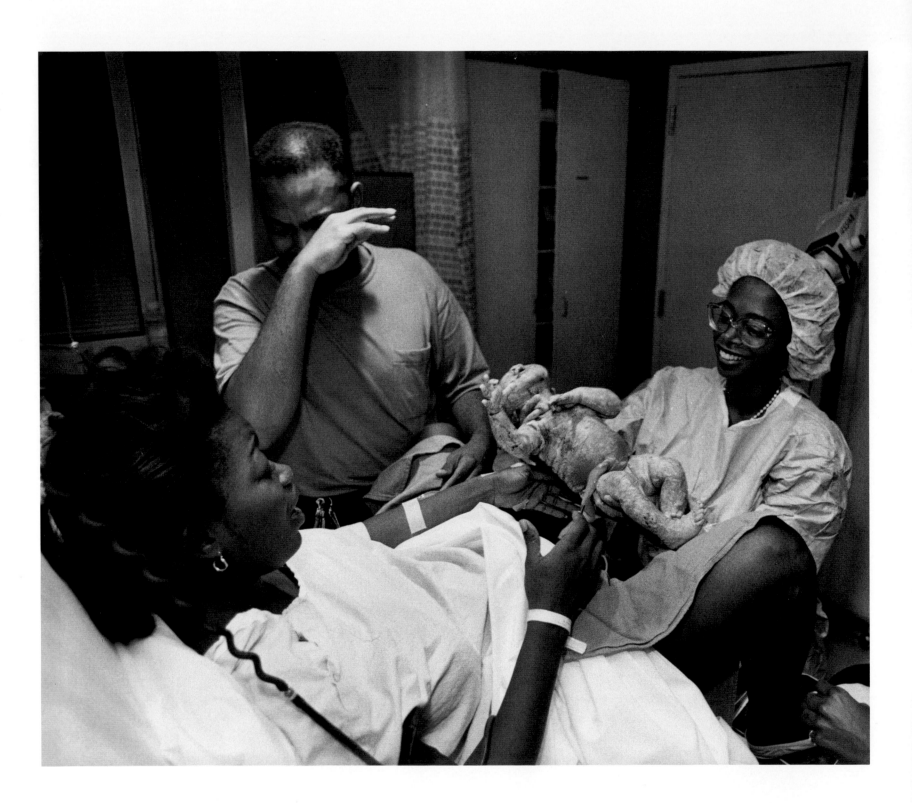

SILVER SPRING, MARYLAND   D. MICHAEL CHEERS

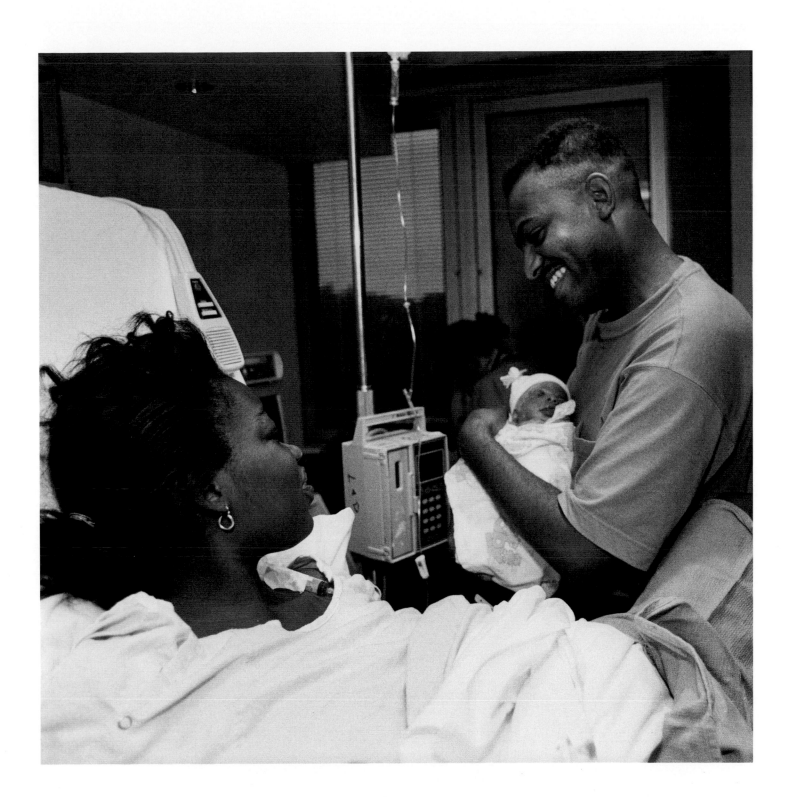

SILVER SPRING, MARYLAND   D. MICHAEL CHEERS

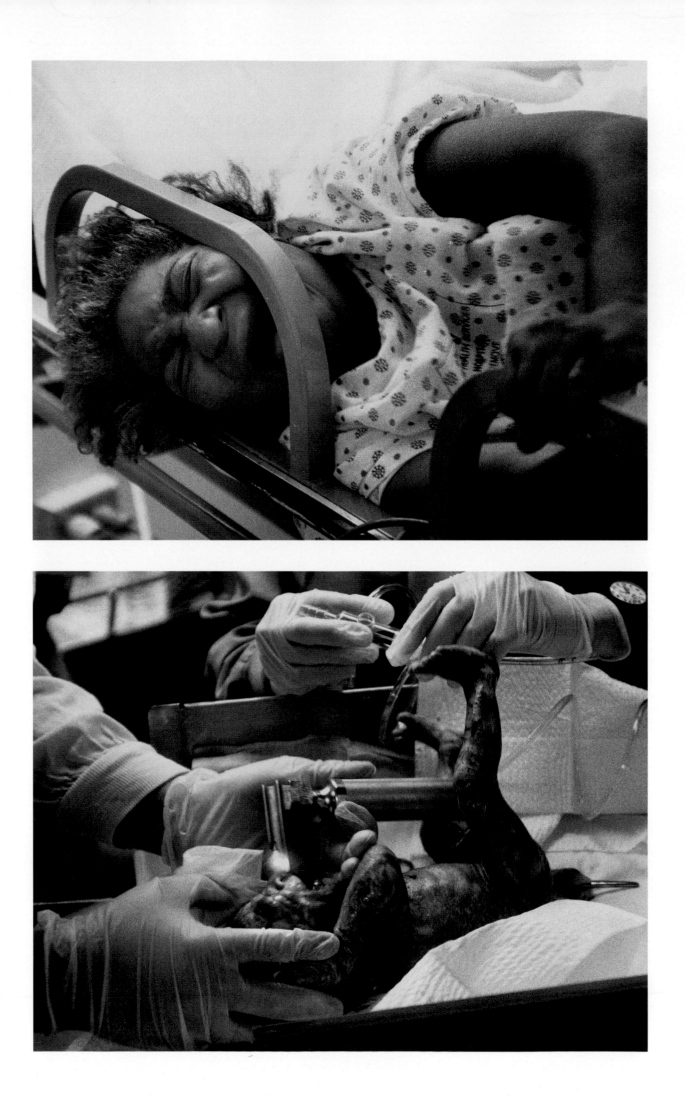

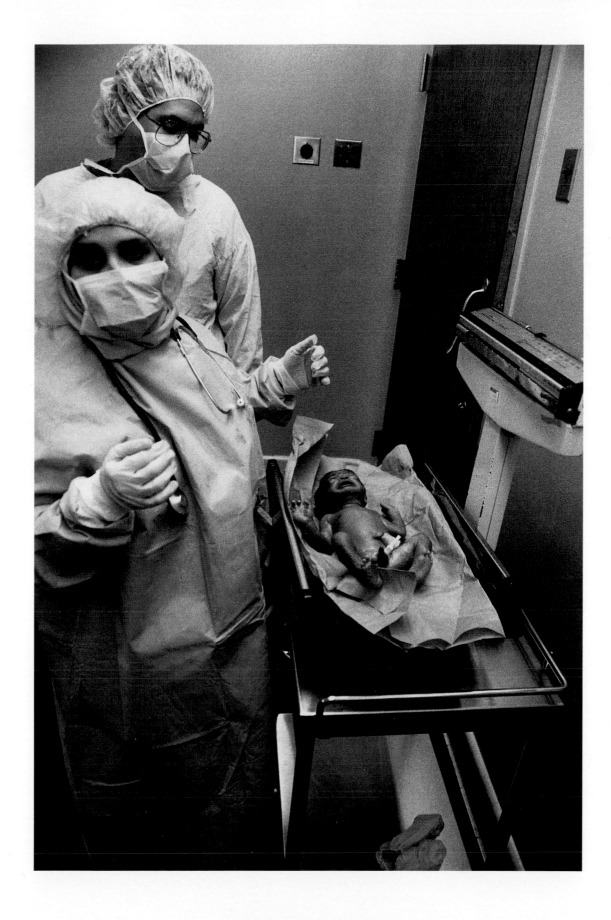

LOS ANGELES, CALIFORNIA

Linda Sattin is an admitted drug abuser who used cocaine, heroine and PCP throughout her pregnancy.

Two days before giving birth to Allen, she smoked crack.

Following a painful delivery, Allen was born—six weeks premature, weighing just over three pounds,

and not breathing. After emergency CPR, Allen was finally revived.

D STEVENS

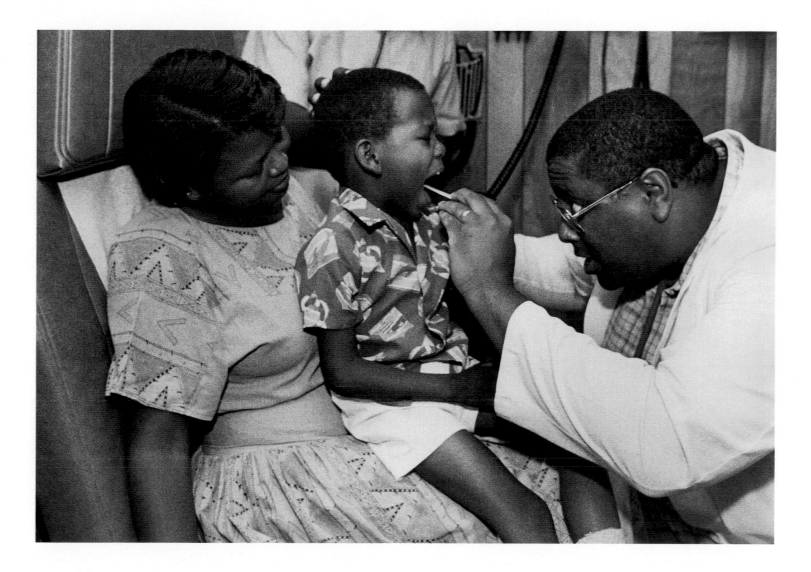

TCHULA, MISSISSIPPI

Country Doctor. When Dr. Ronald Myers decided to bring medicine to rural Mississippi, he was told that Tchula
was "too poor" to support a clinic. With his own money, he transformed an abandoned restaurant
into a family health facility which serves thousands of area residents.
He has kept the clinic open with sparse donations and by working overtime in emergency rooms across the state.
Myers is also an ordained minister and a jazz pianist.

D. MICHAEL CHEERS

< BATON ROUGE, LOUISIANA

A chat in the shade. Lubertha West and her daughter, Georgia Mae Tates.

C. W. GRIFFIN

BEATING THE ODDS

BASSFIELD, MISSISSIPPI

Black farmers lose land at an average of 160,000 acres per year.
Experts predict that by the year 2000 there may be no more Black-
owned and -operated farms in the United States.

JOHN H. WHITE

PETAL, MISSISSIPPI

Workers harvest cucumbers on Ben Burkette's farm.

JOHN H. WHITE

PETAL, MISSISSIPPI

Lesley Brown, four, takes a nap while his mother, Celeste Brown, shucks peas for the evening meal.

JOHN H. WHITE

CARSON, MISSISSIPPI
107-year-old farmer Will Gray watches over his 350 acres.
JOHN H. WHITE

DOOLEY COUNTY, GEORGIA >
Seventy-year-old Tyme Whitehead lives in the house where he was born,
and on the 900 acres that his father acquired nearly 100 years ago.
ROBIN TINAY SALLIE

DOOLEY COUNTY, GEORGIA

Pork is one of Whitehead's biggest money-makers.

ROBIN TINAY SALLIE

DOOLEY COUNTY, GEORGIA

Farmhand Dave Franklin (center) neuters a hog.

He cuts open the sacs, removes the testicles and dabs on burnt motor oil to keep the pigs from bleeding to death.

ROBIN TINAY SALLIE

DOOLEY COUNTY, GEORGIA
The youngest member of the Whitehead clan picks the fruits of his labor.
ROBIN TINAY SALLIE

<   **DOOLEY COUNTY, GEORGIA**
Jimmy Adams hoes weeds from the watermelon patch.
ROBIN TINAY SALLIE

WASHINGTON, D.C.

Muslim girls at Sister Clara Mohammed School have fun during recess.

RON CEASAR

PAWLEY'S ISLAND, SOUTH CAROLINA

Ruby Forsyth, 86, has taught at the Holy Cross Faith Memorial School for 62 years.

She has 60 students, ages 3–10. She teaches pre-school and kindergarten through fourth grade in her one-room schoolhouse.

Forsyth plans to come back next year to dispense her unique blend of love and discipline.

MATTHEW LEWIS

On the blackboard:

Kiswahili

Asante = Thank you
hodi = Asking to enter
Karibou = Welcome
dada = Sister
Ndiyo = yes
Sissi = we
Wa = They
Lakini = but
mama = Mother
mToto = chi

NEW BRUNSWICK, NEW JERSEY
The merit of Afrocentric education is at the forefront of public debate today.
At the private Nyerere Education Institute, high school students are taught Egyptian hieroglyphics and Swahili vocabulary.
CHESTER HIGGINS, JR.

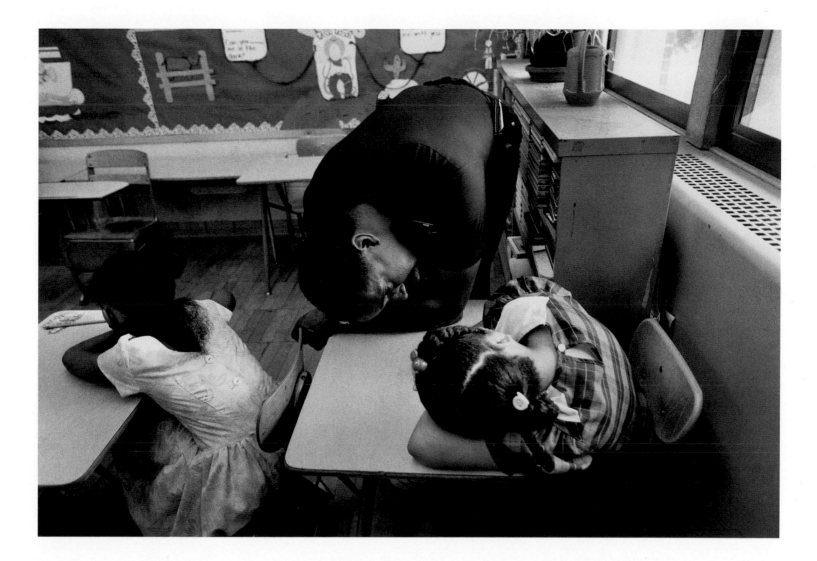

DETROIT, MICHIGAN

One person makes a difference.

Officer Greg Brooks of the Detroit Police Department conducts the Drug Free Schools program at Bow Elementary School.

JACQUES CHENET

ST. HELENA ISLAND, SOUTH CAROLINA

Recognizing the past, Kemba Opio (center) and friends prepare to be the future.

JEFFERY ALLAN SALTER

BALTIMORE, MARYLAND
Investing of the hood at Morgan State University.
DUDLEY M. BROOKS

NEW YORK, NEW YORK   >
Craig Moore, 18, raises pigeons on his Harlem rooftop.
Moore feels that when he's up there, off the streets, he can touch the sky.
BRUCE TALAMON

ACKNOWLEDGMENTS

New African Visions, Inc., expresses our sincere appreciation to those corporations and individuals whose generous contributions made this project possible:

Time Warner

TIME-LIFE Photo Labs

Professional Photography Division, Eastman Kodak Company

The Hitachi Foundation

Carol Randolph, Esq.

Goldfarb, Kaufman and O-Toole

The District of Columbia Commission on the Arts and Humanities

Nelson George, Paula Giddings, Joyce Ladner, Ph.D., Sylvester Monroe

A very special thanks to:

Fredrica S. Friedman, Executive Editor, Little, Brown and Company
Steven J. Ross
Nicholas J. Nicholas
Jerry Levin
Toni Fay
Peter Christopoulos
Hanns Kohl
Billie Jean Lebda
Felicia Lynch
Michael Diamond
Joe Johnson
School of Visual Communications, University of Ohio (Athens)
The Corcoran Gallery of Art
The National Association of Black Journalists
Charles E. Tate
Sharp Advertising

ADVISORY BOARD

Brig. Gen. George M. Brooks,
   (U.S. Army, Ret.)
Lucenia Dunn, Ph.D.
Reginald Dunn
Dorothy Gilliam
Alphonso Jackson
Velma LaPoint, Ph.D.
Barbara Nicholson, Ph.D
Carol Randolph
Lacy Streeter
Ronald Walters, Ph.D.
Samuel F. Yette

NEW AFRICAN VISIONS, INC.

Eric Easter, President
D. Michael Cheers, Vice-President
Dudley M. Brooks, Vice President

SONGS OF MY PEOPLE STAFF

Project Co-Directors:
Eric Easter
D. Michael Cheers
Dudley M. Brooks

Photo Editors:
Dudley M. Brooks
D. Michael Cheers
Michel DuCille
Eric Easter
Vanessa Barnes Hillian
David Lewis
Bryan Monroe

Editorial Coordinator: Harriette Cole

Logistics Coordinator: Vanessa Barnes Hillian

Photo Coordinator: Doug Vann

Research Coordinator: Sandra Gregg

Regional Coordinators:
Deborah Campbell, *West*
Gary J. Kirksey, *Midwest*
Bryan Monroe, *South*
Deirdre Wilson, *Northeast*

Editorial Assistant: Kevin Gibbs

Staff Photographer: Jason Miccolo Johnson

Special thanks to the Brooks and Dyson families as well as my grandparents Herbert and Lucille Hughlett for their constant inspiration. My gratitude to Joseph Elbert, Assistant Managing Editor, *Washington Post* and Michel DuCille, Photo Editor, *Washington Post*; Morgan State University, Cafe Lautrec and University of Maryland Hospital Shock Trauma for their cooperation. Special, special thanks to my wife, Diane, for her constant support.
—Dudley M. Brooks

The Cheers Family—Darline, Imani, D. Michael, Jr., Nia, Milton, Karen and Sharon . . . as well as other friends whose prayers and kindness have sustained me . . Robert Knight, Bob Bailey, Fannie Brown, George E. Curry, Harry Williams, Mike Pfleger, Vickie Pasley, Doris E. Saunders, Cindy Ayers Elliott, Ron S. Rochon, Ladell and Danny Flowers, the Bartley family (Julian, Sue, J.L and Edith), the Clemons family (Ricky, Gail, Jason and Perry), John H. Johnson, Jesse Jackson and Esterline Dean.
—D. Michael Cheers

My gratitude to the Easter, Byrd and Hamilton families, as well as Quincy Jones, Ronald H. Brown, Andrew and Karen Horne, Florence Tate, Kimiko Jackson, Kim Swann, Recoe Walker, Vincenzo Turner, Brian Tate, Rudy Gadsden, T.J. Johnson and Gerald Thompson.
—Eric Easter

PHOTOGRAPHERS

MICHELLE AGINS
New York Times
New York, New York

JULES ALLEN
Freelance Photographer
New York, New York

EARL ANDERSON
Freelance Photographer
New York, New York

**JEANNE
MOUTOUSSAMY-ASHE**
Freelance Photographer
New York, New York

ANTHONY BARBOZA
Freelance Photographer
New York, New York

CONRAD BARCLAY
Freelance Photographer
New York, New York

HOWARD BINGHAM
Freelance Photographer
Los Angeles, California

BOB BLACK
Chicago Sun-Times
Chicago, Illinois

GEARY G. BROADNAX
Houston Post
Houston, Texas

DUDLEY M. BROOKS
Washington Post
Washington, D.C.

RON CEASAR
Freelance Photographer
Washington, D.C.

D. MICHAEL CHEERS
New African Visions, Inc.
Washington, D.C.

JACQUES CHENET
Newsweek
New York, New York

GEORGE CHINSEE
Women's Wear Daily
New York, New York

JAMES V. EVERS
Freelance Photographer
Los Angeles, California

SHARON FARMER
Freelance Photographer
Washington, D.C.

ROLAND L. FREEMAN
Freelance Photographer
Washington, D.C.

VINCE FRYE
Freelance Photographer
New York, New York

MARK GAIL
Fort Worth Star-Telegram
Ft. Worth, Texas

T. ORTEGA GAINES
Charlotte Observer
Charlotte, North Carolina

C. W. GRIFFIN
Miami Herald
Miami, Florida

KEITH HADLEY
Atlanta Constitution
Atlanta, Georgia

DURELL HALL, JR.
Louisville Courier-Journal
Louisville, Kentucky

RENEE HANNANS
Atlanta Constitution
Atlanta, Georgia

CRAIG HERNDON
Washington Post
Washington, D.C.

CHESTER HIGGINS, JR.
New York Times
New York, New York

FRED HUTCHERSON
Rockford Register-Star
Rockford, Illinois

JASON MICCOLO JOHNSON
Freelance Photographer
Washington, D.C.

E. A. KENNEDY, III
Palm Beach Post
West Palm Beach, Florida

DAVID LEE
Freelance Photographer
New York, New York

STEVE LEFKOVITS
USA Today
New York, New York

MATTHEW LEWIS
(retired)
Washington Post
Washington, D.C.

ROY LEWIS
Freelance Photographer
Washington, D.C.

KIRK McKOY
Los Angeles Times
Los Angeles, California

ODELL MITCHELL
St. Louis Post-Dispatch
St. Louis, Missouri

OZIER MUHAMMAD
New York Newsday
New York, New York

MARILYN NANCE
Freelance Photographer
New York, New York

EZIO PETERSON
New York Post
New York, New York

ELI REED
Magnum Photos
New York, New York

MORRIS RICHARDSON
University of Texas, Houston
Houston, Texas

ROBIN TINAY SALLIE
Lexington Herald
Lexington, Kentucky

JEFFERY ALLAN SALTER
New York Newsday
New York, New York

COREEN SIMPSON
Freelance Photographer
New York, New York

LESTER SLOAN
Newsweek
Los Angeles, Californioa

D STEVENS
SIPA Press
Los Angeles, California

BRUCE TALAMON
Freelance Photographer
Los Angeles, California

DIXIE D. VEREEN
USA Today
Arlington, Virginia

KENNETH WALKER
Los Angeles Times
Los Angeles, California

RICARDO WATSON
Freelance Photographer
Washington, D.C.

JIM WELLS
Freelance Photographer
Washington, D.C.

JOHN H. WHITE
Chicago Sun-Times
Chicago, Illinois

KEITH WILLIAMS
Louisville Courier-Journal
Louisville, Kentucky

PAT WEST
Freelance Photographer
Detroit, Michigan

ABOUT THE ESSAYISTS

NELSON GEORGE

is a nationally recognized music critic and the author of several books, including
The Death of Rhythm & Blues (Pantheon, 1988).

PAULA GIDDINGS

is the author of a number of works including *When and Where I Enter: The Impact of Black Women
on Race and Sex in America* (Morrow, 1984).

SYLVESTER MONROE

is a national correspondent for TIME magazine and the co-author of *Brothers: Black and Poor—
A True Story of Courage and Survival* (Morrow, 1988).

JOYCE A. LADNER, Ph.D.

is vice-president for academic affairs at Howard University and the author of a series of books and essays, including
Mixed Families: Adopting Across Racial Boundaries (Anchor Press/Doubleday, 1977).

ABOUT THE EDITORS

ERIC EASTER

is a Washington-based media consultant, writer and producer.

D. MICHAEL CHEERS

is a photojournalist, writer and documentary filmmaker.

DUDLEY M. BROOKS

is an award-winning photojournalist for the *Washington Post*.

DESIGNED BY SUSAN MARSH

PRODUCTION COORDINATED BY CHRISTINA HOLZ ECKERSON

COMPOSITION IN SYNTAX ROMAN BY DEKR CORPORATION

PRINTED AND BOUND BY TIEN WAH PRESS